MW01488044

JESUS REALLY SAID IT

THE WORDS OF JESUS

Compiled by Steve Sandin

PRESS

Contact Steve by e-mail:
jesusreallysaidit@att.net

To Taffy,   July 3, 2013

This is for your family library.
I hope it will inspire your
kids to read and believe what
the Bible says and that God
is truth. John 8:32 says "And
you shall know the truth, and
the truth shall "make you free."
May we all be brave enough to
ask for truth to be revealed
to us in our lives and situations
and then receive God's grace
and help to walk in it! Have
the courage and determination to
share it with others! Steve
did and that's why he wrote
this book.

            Love and Blessings,
            Debbie

John 1:4,9

"In Him was life, and the life was the light of men...
That was the true Light which gives light to every
man coming into the world."

Psalm 119:130

"The entrance of Your words gives light;
It gives understanding to the simple"

Hebrews 13:8

"Jesus Christ is the same yesterday, today,
and forever."

INTRODUCTION

Do you want to know who Jesus is and what He is like? Are you searching for spiritual answers? Perhaps you do not know a pastor, do not have a Bible, or attend a church. If you have questions about Jesus or if you are looking for spiritual truth, keep reading. The words of Jesus are Spirit and Life!

I believe this book is an assignment given to me by God for this time and generation. It is a privilege and honor to serve Him in telling the words of Jesus. This task was not my idea, but given to me by revelation of the Holy Spirit. The Lord told me very clearly,

"People don't know who I truly am. Go through the Gospels and write the words of Jesus and organize them into categories so they will see the relevance of truth and so they will know Jesus."

I believe God wants this book primarily and most importantly in the hands of those who have never heard of Jesus, those who know very little about Him, and those who think they know Jesus but really have not been told the truth. For those who already trust in Jesus and are born again having committed to serve Him, this book will be very encouraging and will provide strength for your faith. It is also a wonderful reference and resource.

The Lord specifically gave each of the categories to me to develop into individual chapters. So I carefully read through all the Gospels of the Holy Bible - Matthew, Mark, Luke, and John. These passages essentially contain all the words recorded by Jesus while He was here on earth. I also read these passages in three different translations - New King James, Amplified, and the New Living Translation. Each verse or passage was selected from one of these translations.

For the parables and passages that are similar accounts in different Gospels, each account will be presented separately. For example, the Parable of the Sower is in Matthew, Mark, and Luke. All three separate accounts were included in the book as a comprehensive representation as some accounts have slight variation and some have principles that may be included in one account but not in another. A different translation may also be found between the accounts. For example, the Matthew account of the Parable of the Sower may be in the New King James while the Mark account may be presented in the Amplified.

This book is not meant to be a comprehensive compilation of all the words of Jesus that were recorded in Scripture or a complete account of His ministry. It is a way to introduce you to Jesus by reading and listening to what He has to say. How do you get to know someone unless you spend time with them? You listen and hear the words they say to understand their thoughts, ideas, philosophies, opinions, and their heart. In this book, Jesus talks about topics and issues that all of us deal with. Some examples are peace, love, forgiveness, healing, salvation, relationships, and conflict resolution. He also discusses eternity and what it means to you and me. Listen to the words of Jesus and let Him speak to you. His words reveal His majesty, wisdom, and glory, but sadly most people don't know who He really is.

Jesus is alive and well and is coming soon. He loves you deeply, bears all of your burdens and concerns, and desires only the very best for you. Jesus wants to be involved in every area of *your* life. He has a lot to say about issues that are relevant to *you* today - relevant to *your* life right now. Let me through this book introduce you to Jesus.

CONTENTS

LOVE

Matthew 5:43-47 "You have heard the law that says, 'Love your neighbor' and hate your enemy. But I say, love your enemies! Pray for those who persecute you! In that way, you will be acting as true children of your Father in heaven. For he gives his sunlight to both the evil and the good, and he sends rain on the just and the unjust alike. If you love only those who love you, what reward is there for that? Even corrupt tax collectors do that much. If you are kind only to your friends, how are you different from anyone else? Even pagans do that." (NLT)

Matthew 22:37-40 "Jesus said to him, 'You shall love the Lord your God with all your heart, with all your soul, and with all your mind.' This is the first and great commandment. And the second is like it: 'You shall love your neighbor as yourself.' On these two commandments hang all the Law and the Prophets." (NKJ)

John 3:16 "For God loved the world so much that he gave his one and only Son, so that everyone who believes in him will not perish but have eternal life." (NLT)

John 13:34-35 "I give you a new commandment: that you should love one another. Just as I have loved you, so you too should love one another. By this shall all [men] know that you are my disciples, if you love one another [if you keep on showing love among yourselves]." (AMP)

John 14:15 "If you love me, keep my commandments." (NKJ)

John 14:21,23-24 "The person who has My commands and keeps them is the one who [really] loves Me; and whoever [really] loves Me will be loved by My Father, and I [too] will love him and will show (reveal, manifest) Myself to him. [I will let myself be clearly seen by him and make Myself real to him]." (AMP)

John 15:9-13,17 "I have loved you, [just] as the Father has loved me; abide in my love [continue in His love with Me]. If you keep my commandments [if you continue to obey my instructions], you will abide in my love and live on in it, just as I have obeyed My Father's commandments and live on in His love. I have told you these things, that My joy and delight may be in you, and that your joy and gladness may be of full measure and complete and overflowing. This is my commandment: that you love one another [just] as I have loved you. No one has greater love [no one has shown stronger affection] than to lay down (give up) his own life for his friends. This is what I command you: that you love one another." (AMP)

John 16:27 "For the Father Himself loves you, because you have loved Me, and have believed that I came forth from God." (NKJ)

FORGIVENESS

Matthew 6:14-15 "If you forgive those who sin against you, your heavenly Father will forgive you. But if you refuse to forgive others, your Father will not forgive your sins." (NLT)

Parable of the Unforgiving Servant

Matthew 18:21-35 "Then Peter came up to Him and said, Lord how many times may my brother sin against me and I forgive him and let it go? [As many as] up to seven times? Jesus answered him, I tell you, not up to seven times, but seventy times seven! Therefore the kingdom of heaven is like a human king who wished to settle accounts with his attendants. When he began the accounting, one was brought to him who owed 10,000 talents [probably about $10,000,000]; And because he could not pay, his master ordered him to be sold, with his wife and his children and everything that he possessed, and payment to be made. So the attendant fell on his knees, begging him, Have patience with me and I will pay you everything. And his master's heart was moved with compassion, and he released him and forgave him [cancelling] the debt.

But that same attendant, as he went out, found one of his fellow attendants who owed him a hundred denarii [about twenty dollars]; and he caught him by the throat and said, Pay what you owe! So his fellow attendant fell down and begged him earnestly, 'Give me time, and I will pay you all!' But he was unwilling, and he went out and had him put in prison till he should pay the debt.

When his fellow attendants saw what had happened, they were greatly distressed, and they went and told everything that had taken place to their master. Then his master called to him and said to him, 'You contemptible and wicked attendant! I forgave and cancelled all that [great] debt of yours because you begged me to. And should you not have had pity and mercy on your fellow attendant, as I had pity and mercy on you?' And in wrath his master turned him over to the torturers (the jailers), till he should pay all that he owed. So also my heavenly Father will deal with every one of you if you do not freely forgive your brother from your heart his offenses." (AMP)

Mark 11:25-26 "And whenever you stand praying, if you have anything against anyone, forgive him and let it drop (leave it, let it go), in order that your Father who is in heaven may also forgive you your [own] failings and shortcomings and let them drop. But if you do not forgive, neither will your Father in heaven forgive your fallings and shortcomings." (AMP)

John 20:23 "If you forgive the sins of any, they are forgiven them; if you retain the sins of any, they are retained." (NKJ)

HEALING

Matthew 8:2-3 "And behold, a leper came up to Him and, prostrating himself, worshipped Him, saying, 'Lord, if you are willing, You are able to cleanse me by curing me.' And He reached out His hand and touched him, saying, I am willing; be cleansed by being cured. And instantly his leprosy was cured and cleansed." (AMP)

Matthew 8:7 "And Jesus said to him, 'I will come and heal him.'" (NKJ)

Matthew 9:22 "But Jesus turned around, and when He saw her He said, 'Be of good cheer, daughter, your faith has made you well.' And the woman was made well from that hour." (NKJ)

Matthew 9:27-30 "When Jesus departed from there, two blind men followed Him, crying out and saying, 'Son of David, have mercy on us!' And when He had come into the house, the blind men came to Him. And Jesus said to them, 'Do you believe that I am able to do this?' They said to Him, 'Yes, Lord.' Then He touched their eyes saying, 'According to your faith let it be to you.' And their eyes were opened." (NKJ)

Matthew11:5 "The blind receive their sight, and the lame walk, lepers are cleansed (by healing) and the deaf hear, the dead are raised up and the poor have good news (the Gospel) preached to them." (AMP)

Mark 1:40-42 "A man with leprosy came and knelt in front of Jesus, begging to be healed. 'If you are willing, you can heal me and make me clean,' he said. Moved with compassion, Jesus reached out and touched him. 'I am willing,' he said. 'Be healed!' Instantly the leprosy disappeared, and the man was healed." (NLT)

Mark 2:9-12 "Which is easier, to say to the paralytic, 'Your sins are forgiven you' or to say, 'Arise, take up your bed and walk'? But that you may know that the Son of Man has the power on earth to forgive sins' - He said to the paralytic, 'I say to you, arise, take up your bed, and go to your house.' Immediately he arose, took up the bed, and went out in the presence of them all, so that all were amazed and glorified God, saying 'We never saw anything like this!" (NKJ)

Mark 5:34 "And He said to her, 'Daughter, your faith (your trust and confidence in Me, springing from faith in God) has restored you to health. Go in (into) peace and be continually healed and freed from your [distressing bodily] disease.'" (AMP)

Mark 5:38-42 "When they came to the home of the synagogue leader, Jesus saw much commotion and weeping and wailing. He went inside and asked, 'Why all this commotion and weeping? The child isn't dead; she's only asleep.' The crowd laughed at him. But he made them all leave, and he took the girl's father and mother and his three disciples into the room where the girl was lying. Holding her hand, he said to her, *'Talitha koum,'* which means 'Little girl, get up!' And the girl, who was twelve years old, immediately stood up and walked around! They were overwhelmed and totally amazed." (NLT)

Mark 7:32-35 "A deaf man with a speech impediment was brought to him, and the people begged Jesus to lay his hands on the man to heal him. Jesus led him away from the crowd so they could be alone. He put his fingers into the man's ears. Then, spitting on his own fingers, he touched the man's tongue. Looking up to heaven, he sighed and said, *'Ephphatha,'* which means, 'Be opened!' Instantly the man could hear perfectly, and his tongue was freed so he could speak plainly!" (NLT)

Mark 10:51-52 "So Jesus answered and said to him, 'What do you want me to do for you?' The blind man said to Him, 'Rabboni, that I may receive my sight.' Then Jesus said to him, 'Go your way; your faith has made you well.' And immediately he received his sight and followed Jesus on the road." (NKJ)

Mark 16:18b "…they will lay their hands on the sick, and they will get well." (AMP)

Luke 5:12-13 "And it happened when He was in a certain city, that behold, a man who was full of leprosy saw Jesus; and he fell on *his* face and implored Him, saying, 'Lord, if You are willing, You can make me clean.' Then He put out *His* hand and touched him, saying, 'I am willing; be cleansed.' Immediately the leprosy left him." (NKJ)

Luke 5:22-23 "But when Jesus perceived their thoughts, He answered and said to them, 'Why are you reasoning in your hearts? Which is easier, to say, your sins are forgiven you, or to say, rise up and walk? But that you may know that the Son of Man has power on earth to forgive sins'—He said to the man who was paralyzed, 'I say to you, arise, take up your bed, and go to your house.' Immediately he rose up before them, took up what he had been lying on, and departed to his own house, glorifying God." (NKJ)

Luke 6:10 "Then He glanced around at them all and said to the man, 'Stretch out your hand!' And he did so, and his hand was fully restored like the other one." (AMP)

Luke 7:12-16 "And when He came near the gate of the city, behold, a dead man was being carried out, the only son of his mother; and she was a widow. And a large crowd from the city was with her. When the Lord saw her, He had compassion on her and said to her, 'Do not weep.' Then He came and touched the open coffin, and those who carried *him* stood still. And He said, 'Young man, I say to you, arise.' So he who was dead sat up and began to speak. And He presented him to his mother. Then fear came upon all, and they glorified God, saying, 'A great prophet has risen up among us'; and, 'God has visited His people.'" (NKJ)

Luke 7:21-22 "In that very hour Jesus was healing many [people] of sicknesses and distressing bodily plagues and evil spirits, and to many who were blind He gave [a free, gracious, joy-giving gift of] sight. So He replied to them, 'Go and tell John what you have seen and heard: the blind receive their sight, the lame walk, the lepers are cleansed, the deaf hear, the dead are raised up, and the poor have the good news (the Gospel) preached to them.'" (AMP)

Luke 8:48 "And He said to her, 'Daughter, your faith (your confidence and trust in Me) has made you well! Go (enter) into peace (untroubled, undisturbed well-being).'" (AMP)

Ten Lepers Cleansed

Luke 17:12-19 "As he entered a village there, ten lepers stood at a distance, crying out, 'Jesus, Master, have mercy on us!' He looked at them and said, 'Go show yourselves to the priests.' And as they went, they were cleansed of their leprosy. One of them, when he saw that he was healed, came back to Jesus, shouting, 'Praise God!' He fell to the ground at Jesus' feet, thanking him for what he had done. This man was a Samaritan. Jesus asked, 'Didn't I heal ten men? Where are the other nine? Has no one returned to give glory to God except this foreigner?' And Jesus said to the man, 'Stand up and go. Your faith has healed you.'" (NLT)

Luke 18:35,40-43 "Then it happened, as He was coming near Jericho, that a certain blind man sat by the road begging. So Jesus stood still and commanded him to be brought to Him. And when he had come near, He asked him, saying, 'What do you want Me to do for you?' He said, 'Lord, that I may receive my sight.' Then Jesus said to him, 'Receive your sight; your faith has made you well.' And immediately he received his sight, and followed Him, glorifying God. And all the people, when they saw *it,* gave praise to God." (NKJ)

John 4:49-51 "The official pleaded, 'Lord, please come now before my little boy dies.'

Then Jesus told him, 'Go back home. Your son will live!' And the man believed what Jesus said and started home.

While the man was on his way, some of his servants met him with the news that his son was alive and well." (NLT)

Man Healed at the Pool of Bethesda

John 5:5-9 "There was a certain man there who had suffered with a deep-seated and lingering disorder for thirty-eight years. When Jesus noticed him lying there [helpless], knowing that he had already been a long time in that condition, He said to him, 'Do you want to become well?' [Are you really in earnest about getting well?] The invalid answered, 'Sir, I have nobody when the water is moving to put me into the pool; but while I am trying to come [into it] myself, somebody else steps down ahead of me.' Jesus said to him, 'Get up! Pick up your bed (sleeping pad) and walk!' Instantly the man became well and recovered his strength and picked up his bed and walked. But that happened on the Sabbath." (AMP)

John 9:1-3 + 6-7 "Now as *Jesus* passed by, He saw a man who was blind from birth. And His disciples asked Him, saying, 'Rabbi, who sinned, this man or his parents, that he was born blind?' Jesus answered, 'Neither this man nor his parents sinned, but that the works of God should be revealed in him'...When He had said these things, He spat on the ground and made clay with the saliva; and He anointed the eyes of the blind man with the clay. And He said to him, 'Go, wash in the pool of Siloam' (which is translated, Sent). So he went and washed, and came back seeing." (NKJ)

John 11:4 "When Jesus received the message, He said, 'This sickness is not to end in death; but [on the contrary] it is to honor God and to promote His glory, that the Son of God may be glorified through (by) it.'" (AMP)

PEACE & REST

Matthew 11:28-30 "Come to Me, all you who labor and are heavy-laden and overburdened, and I will cause you to rest. [I will ease and relieve and refresh your souls.] Take My yoke upon you and learn of Me, for I am gentle (meek) and humble (lowly) in heart, and you will find rest (relief and ease and refreshment and recreation and blessed quiet) for your souls. For My yoke is wholesome (useful, good—not harsh, hard, sharp, or pressing, but comfortable, gracious, and pleasant), and My burden is light and easy to be borne." (AMP)

Matthew 14:27 "But Jesus spoke to them at once. 'Don't be afraid,' he said. 'Take courage. I am here!'" (NLT)

Matthew 17:7 "But Jesus came and touched them and said, 'Arise, and do not be afraid.'" (NKJ)

Mark 4:39 "When Jesus woke up, he rebuked the wind and said to the waves, 'Silence! Be still!' Suddenly the wind stopped, and there was a great calm." (NLT)

Mark 6:31a "Then Jesus said, 'Let's go off by ourselves to a quiet place and rest awhile.'" (NLT)

Luke 6:5 "And He said to them, 'The Son of Man is also Lord of the Sabbath.'" (NKJ)

Luke 10:5-6 "Whatever house you enter, first say, Peace be to this household! [Freedom from all the distresses that result from sin be with this family]. And if anyone [worthy] of peace and blessedness is there, the peace and blessedness you wish shall come upon him; but if not, it shall come back to you." (AMP)

Luke 12:26 "And if worry can't accomplish a little thing like that, what's the use of worrying over bigger things?" (NLT)

Luke 24:36, 38 "Now as they said these things, Jesus Himself stood in the midst of them, and said to them, 'Peace to you.'... And He said to them, 'Why are you troubled? And why do doubts arise in your hearts?' (NKJ)

John 6:20 "But he called out to them, 'Don't be afraid. I am here!'" (NLT)

John 14:1 "Do not let your hearts be troubled (distressed, agitated). You believe in and adhere to and trust in and rely on God; believe in and adhere to and trust in and rely also on Me." (AMP)

John 14:27 "Peace I leave with you, My peace I give to you; not as the world gives do I give to you. Let not your heart be troubled, neither let it be afraid." (NKJ)

John 16:33 "I have told you these things, so that in Me you may have [perfect] peace and confidence. In the world you have tribulation and trials and distress and frustration; but be of good cheer [take courage; be confident, certain, undaunted]! For I have overcome the world. [I have deprived it of power to harm you and have conquered it for you.]" (AMP)

John 20:19-21a "That Sunday evening the disciples were meeting behind locked doors because they were afraid of the Jewish leaders. Suddenly, Jesus was standing there among them! 'Peace be with you,' he said. As he spoke, he

showed them the wounds in his hands and his side. They
were filled with joy when they saw the Lord! Again he said,
'Peace be with you.' (NLT)

SIN, REPENTANCE, & SALVATION

Matthew 4:17 "From that time Jesus began to preach, crying out, Repent (change your mind for the better, heartily amend your ways, with abhorrence of your past sins), for the kingdom of heaven is at hand." (AMP)

Matthew 5:27-30 "You have heard that it was said, you shall not commit adultery. But I say to you that everyone who so much as looks at a woman with evil desire for her has already committed adultery with her in his heart. If your right eye serves as a trap to ensnare you or is an occasion for you to stumble and sin, pluck it out and throw it away. It is better that you lose one of your members than that your whole body be cast into hell (Gehenna). And if your right hand serves as a trap to ensnare you or is an occasion for you to stumble and sin, cut it off and cast it from you. It is better that you lose one of your members than that your entire body should be cast into hell (Gehenna)." (AMP)

Matthew 5:33-37 "Again, you have heard that it was said to the men of old, You shall not swear falsely, but you shall perform your oaths to the Lord [as a religious duty].

But I tell you, Do not bind yourselves by an oath at all: either by heaven, for it is the throne of God; Or by the earth, for it is the footstool of His feet; or by Jerusalem, for it is the city of the Great King. And do not swear by your head, for you are not able to make a single hair white or black. Let your Yes be simply Yes, and your No be simply No; anything more than that comes from the evil one." (AMP)

Matthew 9:13 "But go and learn what *this* means: *'I desire mercy and not sacrifice.'* For I did not come to call the righteous, but sinners, to repentance." (NKJ)

Matthew 15:11,18-20 "It's not what goes into your mouth that defiles you; you are defiled by the words that come out of your mouth...I tell you the truth, until heaven and earth disappear, not even the smallest detail of God's law will disappear until its purpose is achieved. So if you ignore the least commandment and teach others to do the same, you will be called the least in the Kingdom of Heaven. But anyone who obeys God's laws and teaches them will be called great in the Kingdom of Heaven. But I warn you—unless your righteousness is better than the righteousness of the teachers of religious law and the Pharisees, you will never enter the Kingdom of Heaven!" (NLT)

Mark 2:17 "When Jesus heard *it,* He said to them, 'Those who are well have no need of a physician, but those who are sick. I did not come to call *the* righteous, but sinners, to repentance.'" (NKJ)

Mark 7:20-23 "And then he added, 'It is what comes from inside that defiles you. For from within, out of a person's heart, come evil thoughts, sexual immorality, theft, murder, adultery, greed, wickedness, deceit, lustful desires, envy, slander, pride, and foolishness. All these vile things come from within; they are what defile you.'" (NLT)

Luke 5:31-32 "And Jesus replied to them, It is not those who are healthy who need a physician, but those who are sick. I have not come to arouse and invite and call the righteous, but the erring ones (those not free from sin) to repentance [to change their minds for the better and heartily to amend their ways, with abhorrence of their past sins]." (AMP)

Woman With the Alabaster Box

Luke 7:36-48 "One of the Pharisees asked Jesus to have dinner with him, so Jesus went to his home and sat down to eat. When a certain immoral woman from that city heard he was eating there, she brought a beautiful alabaster jar filled with expensive perfume. Then she knelt behind him at his feet, weeping. Her tears fell on his feet, and she wiped them off with her hair. Then she kept kissing his feet and putting perfume on them.

When the Pharisee who had invited him saw this, he said to himself, 'If this man were a prophet, he would know what kind of woman is touching him. She's a sinner!'

Then Jesus answered his thoughts. 'Simon,' he said to the Pharisee, 'I have something to say to you.'

'Go ahead, Teacher,' Simon replied.

Then Jesus told him this story: 'A man loaned money to two people—500 pieces of silver to one and 50 pieces to the other. But neither of them could repay him, so he kindly forgave them both, canceling their debts. Who do you suppose loved him more after that?'

Simon answered, 'I suppose the one for whom he canceled the larger debt.'

'That's right,' Jesus said. Then he turned to the woman and said to Simon, 'Look at this woman kneeling here. When

I entered your home, you didn't offer me water to wash the dust from my feet, but she has washed them with her tears and wiped them with her hair. You didn't greet me with a kiss, but from the time I first came in, she has not stopped kissing my feet. You neglected the courtesy of olive oil to anoint my head, but she has anointed my feet with rare perfume. I tell you, her sins—and they are many—have been forgiven, so she has shown me much love. But a person who is forgiven little shows only little love.' Then Jesus said to the woman, 'Your sins are forgiven.'" (NLT)

Luke 13:1-5 "Just at that time there [arrived] some people who informed Jesus about the Galileans whose blood Pilate had mixed with their sacrifices. And He replied by saying to them, 'Do you think that these Galileans were greater sinners than all the other Galileans because they have suffered in this way? I tell you, No; but unless you repent (change your mind for the better and heartily amend your ways, with abhorrence of your past sins), you will all likewise perish and be lost eternally. Or those eighteen on whom the tower in Siloam fell and killed them—do you think that they were more guilty offenders (debtors) than all the others who dwelt in Jerusalem? I tell you, No; but unless you repent (change your mind for the better and heartily amend your ways, with abhorrence of your past sins), you will all likewise perish and be lost eternally.'" (AMP)

Parable of the Lost Sheep

Luke 15:4-7 "What man of you, having a hundred sheep, if he loses one of them, does not leave the ninety-nine in the wilderness, and go after the one which is lost until he finds it? And when he has found *it,* he lays *it* on his shoulders, rejoicing. And when he comes home, he calls together *his* friends and neighbors, saying to them, 'Rejoice with me, for I have found my sheep which was lost!' I say to you that likewise there will be more joy in heaven over one sinner who repents than over ninety-nine just persons who need no repentance." (NKJ)

Parable of the Lost Coin

Luke 15:8-10 "Or what woman, having ten silver coins, if she loses one coin, does not light a lamp, sweep the house, and search carefully until she finds *it?* And when she has found *it,* she calls *her* friends and neighbors together, saying, 'Rejoice with me, for I have found the piece which I lost!' Likewise, I say to you, there is joy in the presence of the angels of God over one sinner who repents." (NKJ)

Parable of the Prodigal Son

Luke 15:11-32 "To illustrate the point further, Jesus told them this story: A man had two sons. The younger son told his father, 'I want my share of your estate now before you die.' So his father agreed to divide his wealth between his

sons. A few days later this younger son packed all his belongings and moved to a distant land, and there he wasted all
his money in wild living. About the time his money ran out,
a great famine swept over the land, and he began to starve.
He persuaded a local farmer to hire him, and the man sent
him into his fields to feed the pigs. The young man became
so hungry that even the pods he was feeding the pigs looked
good to him. But no one gave him anything.

When he finally came to his senses, he said to himself,
'At home even the hired servants have food enough to
spare, and here I am dying of hunger! I will go home to my
father and say, Father, I have sinned against both heaven
and you, and I am no longer worthy of being called your
son. Please take me on as a hired servant.' So he returned
home to his father. And while he was still a long way off, his
father saw him coming. Filled with love and compassion, he
ran to his son, embraced him, and kissed him. His son said
to him, 'Father, I have sinned against both heaven and you,
and I am no longer worthy of being called your son.' But his
father said to the servants, 'Quick! Bring the finest robe in
the house and put it on him. Get a ring for his finger and
sandals for his feet. And kill the calf we have been fattening.
We must celebrate with a feast, for this son of mine was
dead and has now returned to life. He was lost, but now
he is found.' So the party began. Meanwhile, the older son
was in the fields working. When he returned home, he heard
music and dancing in the house, and he asked one of the
servants what was going on. 'Your brother is back,' he was
told, 'and your father has killed the fattened calf. We are

celebrating because of his safe return.' The older brother was angry and wouldn't go in. His father came out and begged him, but he replied, 'All these years I've slaved for you and never once refused to do a single thing you told me to. And in all that time you never gave me even one young goat for a feast with my friends. Yet when this son of yours comes back after squandering your money on prostitutes, you celebrate by killing the fattened calf!' His father said to him, 'Look, dear son, you have always stayed by me, and everything I have is yours. We had to celebrate this happy day. For your brother was dead and has come back to life! He was lost, but now he is found!'" (NLT)

Luke 24:46-47 "Then He said to them, 'Thus it is written, and thus it was necessary for the Christ to suffer and to rise from the dead the third day, and that repentance and remission of sins should be preached in His name to all nations, beginning at Jerusalem.'" (NKJ)

John 3:3-8 "Jesus answered and said to him, 'Most assuredly, I say to you, unless one is born again, he cannot see the kingdom of God.' Nicodemus said to Him, 'How can a man be born when he is old? Can he enter a second time into his mother's womb and be born?' Jesus answered, 'Most assuredly, I say to you, unless one is born of water and the Spirit, he cannot enter the kingdom of God. That which is born of the flesh is flesh, and that which is born of the Spirit is spirit. Do not marvel that I said to you, 'You must be born again.' The wind blows where it wishes, and you hear the sound of it, but cannot tell where it comes from and where it goes. So is everyone who is born of the Spirit.'" (NKJ)

John 3:17 "For God did not send His Son into the world to condemn the world, but that the world through Him might be saved." (NKJ)

John 5:12-14 "They asked him, 'Who is the Man who told you, pick up your bed and walk?' Now the invalid who had been healed did not know who it was, for Jesus had quietly gone away [had passed on unnoticed], since there was a crowd in the place.

Afterward, when Jesus found him in the temple, He said to him, 'See, you are well! Stop sinning or something worse may happen to you.'" (AMP)

John 5:24 "I tell you the truth, those who listen to my message and believe in God who sent me have eternal life. They will never be condemned for their sins, but they have already passed from death into life." (NLT)

John 6:40 "And this is the will of Him who sent Me, that everyone who sees the Son and believes in Him may have everlasting life; and I will raise him up at the last day." (NKJ)

John 6:47 "I assure you, most solemnly I tell you, he who believes in Me [who adheres to, trusts in, relies on, and has faith in Me] has (now possesses) eternal life." (AMP)

Woman Caught In Adultery

John 8:3-11 "Then the scribes and Pharisees brought to Him a woman caught in adultery. And when they had set her in the midst, they said to Him, 'Teacher, this woman was caught in adultery, in the very act. Now Moses, in the law, commanded us that such should be stoned. But what do You say?' This they said, testing Him, that they might have *something* of which to accuse Him. But Jesus stooped down and wrote on the ground with *His* finger, as though He did not hear. So when they continued asking Him, He raised Himself up and said to them, 'He who is without sin among you, let him throw a stone at her first.' And again He stooped down and wrote on the ground. Then those who heard *it,* being convicted by *their* conscience, went out one by one, beginning with the oldest *even* to the last. And Jesus was left alone, and the woman standing in the midst. When Jesus had raised Himself up and saw no one but the woman, He said to her, 'Woman, where are those accusers of yours? Has no one condemned you?' She said, 'No one, Lord.' And Jesus said to her, 'Neither do I condemn you; go and sin no more.'" (NKJ)

John 8:23-24 "He said to them, You are from below; I am from above. You are of this world (of this earthly order); I am not of this world. That is why I told you that you will die in (under the curse of) your sins; for if you do not believe that I am He [Whom I claim to be—if you do not adhere to, trust in, and rely on Me], you will die in your sins." (AMP)

John 8:34 "Jesus answered them, I assure you, most solemnly I tell you, Whoever commits and practices sin is the slave of sin." (AMP)

John 10:27-29 "My sheep hear My voice, and I know them, and they follow Me. And I give them eternal life, and they shall never perish; neither shall anyone snatch them out of My hand. My Father, who has given *them* to Me, is greater than all; and no one is able to snatch *them* out of My Father's hand." (NKJ)

John 11:25-26 "Jesus said to her, "I am the resurrection and the life. He who believes in Me, though he may die, he shall live. And whoever lives and believes in Me shall never die. Do you believe this?" (NKJ)

John 15:22-24 "They would not be guilty if I had not come and spoken to them. But now they have no excuse for their sin. Anyone who hates me also hates my Father. If I hadn't done such miraculous signs among them that no one else could do, they would not be guilty. But as it is, they have seen everything I did, yet they still hate me and my Father." (NLT)

DELIVERANCE

Matthew 12:25-29 "But Jesus knew their thoughts, and said to them: Every kingdom divided against itself is brought to desolation, and every city or house divided against itself will not stand. If Satan casts out Satan, he is divided against himself. How then will his kingdom stand? And if I cast out demons by Beelzebub, by whom do your sons cast *them* out? Therefore they shall be your judges. But if I cast out demons by the Spirit of God, surely the kingdom of God has come upon you. Or how can one enter a strong man's house and plunder his goods, unless he first binds the strong man? And then he will plunder his house.'" (NKJ)

Matthew 12:43-45 "When an unclean spirit goes out of a man, he goes through dry places, seeking rest, and finds none. Then he says, 'I will return to my house from which I came.' And when he comes, he finds *it* empty, swept, and put in order. Then he goes and takes with him seven other spirits more wicked than himself, and they enter and dwell there; and the last *state* of that man is worse than the first. So shall it also be with this wicked generation." (NKJ)

Matthew 17:21 "But this kind does not go out except by prayer and fasting." (AMP)

Mark 1:25-26 "Jesus cut him short. 'Be quiet! Come out of the man,' he ordered. At that, the evil spirit screamed, threw the man into a convulsion, and then came out of him." (NLT)

Mark 3:23-30 "So He called them to *Himself* and said to them in parables: How can Satan cast out Satan. If a kingdom is divided against itself, that kingdom cannot stand. And if a house is divided against itself, that house cannot stand. And if Satan has risen up against himself, and is divided, he cannot stand, but has an end. No one can enter a strong man's house and plunder his goods, unless he first binds the strong man. And then he will plunder his house. Assuredly, I say to you, all sins will be forgiven the sons of men, and whatever blasphemies they may utter; but he who blasphemes against the Holy Spirit never has forgiveness, but is subject to eternal condemnation'— because they said, 'He has an unclean spirit.'" (NKJ)

Mark 5:7-8 "And crying out with a loud voice, he said, 'What have You to do with me, Jesus, Son of the Most High God? [What is there in common between us?] I solemnly implore you by God, do not begin to torment me!' For Jesus was commanding, 'Come out of the man, you unclean spirit!'" (AMP)

Mark 7:29-30 "And He said to her, Because of this saying, you may go your way; the demon has gone out of your daughter [permanently]. And she went home and found the child thrown on the couch, and the demon departed." (AMP)

Mark 9:25-29 "When Jesus saw that the people came running together, He rebuked the unclean spirit, saying to it, 'Deaf and dumb spirit, I command you, come out of him and enter him no more!' Then *the spirit* cried out, convulsed him greatly, and came out of him. And he became as one dead, so that many said, 'He is dead.' But Jesus took him by the hand and lifted him up, and he arose. And when He had come into the house, His disciples asked Him privately, 'Why could we not cast it out?' So He said to them, 'This kind can come out by nothing but prayer and fasting.'" (NKJ)

Mark 16:17-18a "And these signs will follow those who believe: In My name they will cast out demons; they will speak with new tongues; they will take up serpents; and if they drink anything deadly, it will by no means hurt them;" (NKJ)

Luke 4:35 "Jesus cut him short. 'Be quiet! Come out of the man,' he ordered. At that, the demon threw the man to the floor as the crowd watched; then it came out of him without hurting him further." (NLT)

Luke 9:41-42 "Jesus answered, 'O [faithless ones] unbelieving and without trust in God, a perverse (wayward, crooked and warped) generation! Until when and how long am I to be with you and bear with you? Bring your son here [to Me].' And even while he was coming, the demon threw him down and [completely] convulsed him. But Jesus censured and severely rebuked the unclean spirit and healed the child and restored him to his father." (AMP)

Luke 10:18-20 "And He said to them, 'I saw Satan fall like lightning from heaven. Behold, I give you the authority to trample on serpents and scorpions, and over all the power of the enemy, and nothing shall by any means hurt you. Nevertheless do not rejoice in this, that the spirits are subject to you, but rather rejoice because your names are written in heaven.'" (NKJ)

Luke 11:17-26 "He knew their thoughts, so he said, 'Any kingdom divided by civil war is doomed. A family splintered by feuding will fall apart. You say I am empowered by Satan. But if Satan is divided and fighting against himself, how can his kingdom survive? And if I am empowered by Satan, what about your own exorcists? They cast out demons, too, so they will condemn you for what you have said. But if I am casting out demons by the power of God, then the Kingdom of God has arrived among you. For when a strong man like Satan is fully armed and guards his palace, his possessions are safe— until someone even stronger attacks and overpowers him, strips him of his weapons, and carries off his belongings. Anyone who isn't with me opposes me, and anyone who isn't working with me is actually working against me. When an evil spirit leaves a person, it goes into the desert, searching for rest. But when it finds none, it says, 'I will return to the person I came from.' So it returns and finds that its former home is all swept and in order. Then the spirit finds seven other spirits more evil than itself, and they all enter the person and live there. And so that person is worse off than before.'" (NLT)

Luke 13:11-13,16 "He saw a woman who had been crippled by an evil spirit. She had been bent double for eighteen years and was unable to stand up straight. When Jesus saw her, he called her over and said, 'Dear woman, you are healed of your sickness!' Then he touched her, and instantly she could stand straight. How she praised God!... This dear woman, a daughter of Abraham, has been held in bondage by Satan for eighteen years. Isn't it right that she be released, even on the Sabbath?" (NLT)

Luke 22:31-32 "Simon, Simon (Peter), listen! Satan has asked excessively that [all of] you be given up to him [out of the power and keeping of God], that he might sift [all of] you like grain, But I have prayed especially for you [Peter], that your [own] faith may not fail; and when you yourself have turned again, strengthen and establish your brethren." (AMP)

RELIGOUS TRADITION

Matthew 12:7-8 "And if you had only known what this saying means, 'I desire mercy [readiness to help, to spare, to forgive] rather than sacrifice and sacrificial victims, you would not have condemned the guiltless.' For the Son of Man is Lord [even] of the Sabbath." (AMP)

Matthew 12:11-12 "But He said to them, 'What man is there among you, if he has only one sheep and it falls into a pit or ditch on the Sabbath, will not take hold of it and lift it out? How much better and of more value is a man than a sheep! So it is lawful and allowable to do good on the Sabbath days.'" (AMP)

Matthew 13:52 "Then he added, 'Every teacher of religious law who becomes a disciple in the Kingdom of Heaven is like a homeowner who brings from his storeroom new gems of truth as well as old.'" (NLT)

Matthew 15:3-9 "He replied to them, 'And why also do you transgress and violate the commandment of God for the sake of the rules handed down to you by your forefathers (the elders)? For God commanded, Honor your father and your mother, and He who curses or reviles or speaks evil of or abuses or treats improperly his father or mother, let him surely come to his end by death.' But you say, if anyone tells his father or mother, 'What you would have gained from me [that is, the money and whatever I have that might be used for helping you] is already dedicated as a gift to God', then he is exempt and no longer under obligation to honor and help his father or his mother. So for the sake of your tradition (the rules handed down by your forefathers), you have set aside the Word of God [depriving it of force and authority and making it of no effect]. You pretenders (hypocrites)! Admirably and truly did Isaiah prophesy of you when he said: 'These people draw near Me with their mouths and honor Me with their lips, but their hearts hold off and are far away from Me. Uselessly do they worship Me, for they teach as doctrines the commands of men.'" (AMP)

Matthew 21:12-13 "Then Jesus went into the temple of God and drove out all those who bought and sold in the temple, and overturned the tables of the money changers and the seats of those who sold doves. And He said to them, 'It is written, *'My house shall be called a house of prayer,'* but you have made it a *'den of thieves.'"* (NKJ)

Matthew 23:1-7 "Then Jesus said to the multitudes and to His disciples, 'The scribes and Pharisees sit on Moses' seat [of authority]. So observe and practice all they tell you; but do not do what they do, for they preach, but do not practice. They tie up heavy loads, hard to bear, and place them on men's shoulders, but they themselves will not lift a finger to help bear them. They do all their works to be seen of men; for they make wide their phylacteries (small cases enclosing certain Scripture passages, worn during prayer on the left arm and forehead) and make long their fringes [worn by all male Israelites, according to the command]. And they take pleasure in and [thus] love the place of honor at feasts and the best seats in the synagogues and to be greeted with honor in the marketplaces and to have people call them Rabbi.'" (AMP)

Matthew 23:13-36 "What sorrow awaits you teachers of religious law and you Pharisees. Hypocrites! For you shut the door of the Kingdom of Heaven in people's faces. You won't go in yourselves, and you don't let others enter either. What sorrow awaits you teachers of religious law and you Pharisees. Hypocrites! For you cross land and sea to make one convert, and then you turn that person into twice the child of hell you yourselves are! Blind guides!

What sorrow awaits you! For you say that it means nothing to swear 'by God's Temple,' but that it is binding to swear 'by the gold in the Temple.' Blind fools! Which is more important—the gold or the Temple that makes the gold sacred? And you say that to swear 'by the altar' is not binding, but to swear 'by the gifts on the altar' is binding. How blind! For which is more important—the gift on the altar or the altar that makes the gift sacred? When you swear 'by the altar,' you are swearing by it and by everything on it. And when you swear 'by the Temple,' you are swearing by it and by God, who lives in it. And when you swear 'by heaven,' you are swearing by the throne of God and by God, who sits on the throne.

What sorrow awaits you teachers of religious law and you Pharisees. Hypocrites! For you are careful to tithe even the tiniest income from your herb gardens, but you ignore the more important aspects of the law—justice, mercy, and faith. You should tithe, yes, but do not neglect the more important things. Blind guides! You strain your water so you won't accidentally swallow a gnat, but you swallow a camel!

What sorrow awaits you teachers of religious law and you Pharisees. Hypocrites! For you are so careful to clean the outside of the cup and the dish, but inside you are filthy—full of greed and self-indulgence! You blind Pharisee! First wash the inside of the cup and the dish, and then the outside will become clean, too.

What sorrow awaits you teachers of religious law and you Pharisees. Hypocrites! For you are like whitewashed tombs—beautiful on the outside but filled on the inside with dead people's bones and all sorts of impurity. Outwardly you look like righteous people, but inwardly your hearts are filled with hypocrisy and lawlessness.

What sorrow awaits you teachers of religious law and you Pharisees. Hypocrites! For you build tombs for the prophets your ancestors killed, and you decorate the monuments of the godly people your ancestors destroyed. Then you say, 'If we had lived in the days of our ancestors, we would never have joined them in killing the prophets.' But in saying that, you testify against yourselves that you are indeed the descendants of those who murdered the prophets. Go ahead and finish what your ancestors started. Snakes! Sons of vipers! How will you escape the judgment of hell?

Therefore, I am sending you prophets and wise men and teachers of religious law. But you will kill some by crucifixion, and you will flog others with whips in your syna-gogues, chasing them from city to city. As a result, you will be held responsible for the murder of all godly people of all time—from the murder of righteous Abel to the murder of Zechariah son of Barachiah, whom you killed in the Temple between the sanctuary and the altar. I tell you the truth, this judgment will fall on this very generation." (NLT)

Mark 2:25-28 "But He said to them, 'Have you never read what David did when he was in need and hungry, he and those with him: how he went into the house of God *in the days* of Abiathar the high priest, and ate the showbread, which is not lawful to eat except for the priests, and also gave some to those who were with him?' And He said to them, 'The Sabbath was made for man, and not man for the Sabbath. Therefore the Son of Man is also Lord of the Sabbath.'" (NKJ)

Mark 7:6-13 "He answered and said to them, 'Well did Isaiah prophesy of you hypocrites, as it is written:

'This people honors Me with their lips,
But their heart is far from Me.
And in vain they worship Me,
Teaching as doctrines the commandments of men.'

For laying aside the commandment of God, you hold the tradition of men—the washing of pitchers and cups, and many other such things you do.' He said to them, '*All too* well you reject the commandment of God, that you may keep your tradition. For Moses said, '*Honor your father and your mother*'; and, '*He who curses father or mother, let him be put to death.*' But you say, 'If a man says to his father or

46

mother, 'Whatever profit you might have received from me *is* Corban'—' (that is, a gift *to God*), then you no longer let him do anything for his father or his mother, making the word of God of no effect through your tradition which you have handed down. And many such things you do.'" (NKJ)

Mark 11:17 "And He taught and said to them, 'Is it not written, My house shall be called a house of prayer for all the nations? But you have turned it into a den of robbers.'" (AMP)

Mark 12:38-40 "Jesus also taught: 'Beware of these teachers of religious law! For they like to parade around in flowing robes and receive respectful greetings as they walk in the marketplaces. And how they love the seats of honor in the synagogues and the head table at banquets. Yet they shamelessly cheat widows out of their property and then pretend to be pious by making long prayers in public. Because of this, they will be more severely punished.'" (NLT)

Luke 6:9 "Then Jesus said to them, 'I will ask you one thing: Is it lawful on the Sabbath to do good or to do evil, to save life or to destroy?'" (NKJ)

Luke 11:39-52 "Then the Lord said to him, 'Now you Pharisees make the outside of the cup and dish clean, but your inward part is full of greed and wickedness. Foolish ones! Did not He who made the outside make the inside also? But rather give alms of such things as you have; then indeed all things are clean to you. But woe to you Pharisees! For you tithe mint and rue and all manner of herbs, and pass by justice and the love of God. These you ought to have done, without leaving the others undone. Woe to you Pharisees! For you love the best seats in the synagogues and greetings in the marketplaces. Woe to you, scribes and Pharisees, hypocrites! For you are like graves which are not seen, and the men who walk over *them* are not aware *of them.*' Then one of the lawyers answered and said to Him, 'Teacher, by saying these things You reproach us also.' And He said, 'Woe to you also, lawyers! For you load men with burdens hard to bear, and you yourselves do not touch the burdens with one of your fingers. Woe to you! For you build the tombs of the prophets, and your fathers killed them. In fact, you bear witness that you approve the deeds of your fathers; for they indeed killed them, and you build their tombs.' Therefore the wisdom of God also said, 'I will send them prophets and apostles, and *some* of them they will kill and persecute,' that the blood of all the prophets which was shed from the foundation of the world may be required of this generation, from the blood of Abel to the blood of Zechariah who perished between the altar and the temple. Yes, I say to you, it shall be required of this generation. Woe to you lawyers! For you have taken away the key of knowledge. You did not enter in yourselves, and those who were entering in you hindered.'" (NKJ)

Luke 12:54-56 "Then He also said to the multitudes, 'Whenever *you see* a cloud rising out of the west, immediately you say, 'A shower is coming'; and so it is. And when *you see* the south wind blow, you say, 'There will be hot weather'; and there is. Hypocrites! You can discern the face of the sky and of the earth, but how *is it* you do not discern this time?'" (NKJ)

Luke 16:15 "But He said to them, 'You are the ones who declare yourselves just and upright before men, but God knows your hearts. For what is exalted and highly thought of among men is detestable and abhorrent (an abomination) in the sight of God.'" (AMP)

Parable of the Pharisee & Tax Collector

Luke 18:10-14 "Two men went to the Temple to pray. One was a Pharisee, and the other was a despised tax collector. The Pharisee stood by himself and prayed this prayer: I thank you, God, that I am not a sinner like everyone else. For I don't cheat, I don't sin, and I don't commit adultery. I'm certainly not like that tax collector! I fast twice a week, and I give you a tenth of my income.' But the tax collector stood at a distance and dared not even lift his eyes to heaven as he prayed. Instead, he beat his chest in sorrow, saying, 'O God, be merciful to me, for I am a sinner.' I tell you, this sinner, not the Pharisee, returned home justified before God. For those who exalt themselves will be humbled, and those who humble themselves will be exalted." (NLT)

Luke 19:46-46 "Then Jesus entered the Temple and began to drive out the people selling animals for sacrifices. He said to them, 'The Scriptures declare, 'My Temple will be a house of prayer,' but you have turned it into a den of thieves.'" (NLT)

Luke 20:46-47 "Beware of the scribes, who like to walk about in long robes and love to be saluted [with honor] in places where people congregate and love the front and best seats in the synagogues and places of distinction at feasts, who make away with and devour widows' houses, and [to cover it up] with pretense make long prayers. They will receive the greater condemnation (the heavier sentence, the severer punishment)." (AMP)

John 5:38-47 "But you do not have His word abiding in you, because whom He sent, Him you do not believe. You search the Scriptures, for in them you think you have eternal life; and these are they which testify of Me. But you are not willing to come to Me that you may have life. I do not receive honor from men. But I know you, that you do not have the love of God in you. I have come in My Father's name, and you do not receive Me; if another comes in his own name, him you will receive. How can you believe, who receive honor from one another, and do not seek the honor that *comes* from the only God? Do not think that I shall accuse you to the Father; there is *one* who accuses you—Moses, in whom you trust. For if you believed Moses, you would believe Me; for he wrote about Me. But if you do not believe his writings, how will you believe My words?" (NKJ)

John 7:22-24 "Moses therefore gave you circumcision (not that it is from Moses, but from the fathers), and you circumcise a man on the Sabbath. If a man receives circumcision on the Sabbath, so that the law of Moses should not be broken, are you angry with Me because I made a man completely well on the Sabbath? Do not judge according to appearance, but judge with righteous judgment." (NKJ)

John 8:13-15 "Whereupon the Pharisees told Him, You are testifying on Your own behalf; Your testimony is not valid and is worthless. Jesus answered, 'Even if I do testify on My own behalf, My testimony is true and reliable and valid, for I know where I came from and where I am going; but you do not know where I come from or where I am going. You [set yourselves up to] judge according to the flesh (by what you see). [You condemn by external, human standards.] I do not [set Myself up to] judge or condemn or sentence anyone.'" (AMP)

John 8:19 "Then they said to Him, 'Where is this Father of Yours? Jesus answered,'You know My Father as little as you know Me. If you knew Me, you would know My Father also.'" (AMP)

John 8:39-47 "'Our father is Abraham!' they declared. 'No,' Jesus replied, 'for if you were really the children of Abraham, you would follow his example. Instead, you are trying to kill me because I told you the truth, which I heard from God. Abraham never did such a thing. No, you are imitating your real father.' They replied, 'We aren't illegitimate children! God himself is our true Father.' Jesus told them, 'If God were your Father, you would love me, because I have come to you from God. I am not here on my own, but he sent me. Why can't you understand what I am saying? It's because you can't even hear me! For you are the children of your father the devil, and you love to do the evil things he does. He was a murderer from the beginning. He has always hated the truth, because there is no truth in him. When he lies, it is consistent with his character; for he is a liar and the father of lies. So when I tell the truth, you just naturally don't believe me! Which of you can truthfully accuse me of sin? And since I am telling you the truth, why don't you believe me? Anyone who belongs to God listens gladly to the words of God. But you don't listen because you don't belong to God.'" (NLT)

John 8:54-55 "Jesus answered, If I were to glorify Myself (magnify, praise, and honor Myself), I would have no real glory, for My glory would be nothing and worthless. [My honor must come to Me from My Father.] It is My Father Who glorifies Me [Who extols Me, magnifies, and praises Me], of Whom you say that He is your God. Yet you do not know Him or recognize Him and are not acquainted with Him, but I know Him. If I should say that I do not know Him, I would be a liar like you. But I know Him and keep His word [obey His teachings, am faithful to His message]." (AMP)

John 9:39-41 "'Then Jesus said, 'I came into this world for judgment [as a Separator, in order that there may be separation between those who believe on Me and those who reject Me], to make the sightless see and to make those who see become blind.' Some Pharisees who were near, hearing this remark, said to Him, 'Are we also blind?' Jesus said to them, 'If you were blind, you would have no sin; but because you now claim to have sight, your sin remains.' [If you were blind, you would not be guilty of sin; but because you insist, We do see clearly, you are unable to escape your guilt.]" (AMP)

John 10:24-26 "The people surrounded him and asked, 'How long are you going to keep us in suspense? If you are the Messiah, tell us plainly.' Jesus replied, 'I have already told you, and you don't believe me. The proof is the work I do in my Father's name. But you don't believe me because you are not my sheep.'" (NLT)

FAITH

Matthew 8:13 "Then Jesus said to the centurion, "Go your way; and as you have believed, *so* let it be done for you.' And his servant was healed that same hour." (NKJ)

Matthew 9:29 "Then he touched their eyes and said, 'Because of your faith, it will happen.'" (NLT)

Matthew 14:31 "Instantly Jesus reached out His hand and caught and held him, saying to him, 'O you of little faith, why did you doubt?'" (AMP)

Matthew 15:28 "Then Jesus answered her, 'O woman, great is your faith! Be it done for you as you wish.' And her daughter was cured from that moment." (AMP)

Matthew 21:21 "And Jesus answered them, 'Truly I say to you, if you have faith (a firm relying trust) and do not doubt, you will not only do what has been done to the fig tree, but even if you say to this mountain, 'Be taken up and cast into the sea', it will be done.'" (AMP)

Mark 9:23 "Jesus said to him, 'If you can believe, all things *are* possible to him who believes.'" (NKJ)

Mark 10:27 "But Jesus looked at them and said, 'With men *it is* impossible, but not with God; for with God all things are possible.'" (NKJ)

Luke 7:50 "But Jesus said to the woman, 'Your faith has saved you; go (enter) into peace' [in freedom from all the distresses that are experienced as the result of sin]." (AMP)

Luke 17:6 "So the Lord said, 'If you have faith as a mustard seed, you can say to this mulberry tree, 'Be pulled up by the roots and be planted in the sea,' and it would obey you.'" (NKJ)

Luke 18:27 "But He said, 'The things which are impossible with men are possible with God.' (NKJ)

John 11:40 "Jesus said to her, 'Did I not tell you and promise you that if you would believe and rely on Me, you would see the glory of God?'" (AMP)

WORK

Luke 12:15-21 "Then he said, 'Beware! Guard against every kind of greed. Life is not measured by how much you own.' Then he told them a story: A rich man had a fertile farm that produced fine crops. He said to himself, 'What should I do? I don't have room for all my crops.' Then he said, 'I know! I'll tear down my barns and build bigger ones. Then I'll have room enough to store all my wheat and other goods. And I'll sit back and say to myself, my friend, you have enough stored away for years to come. Now take it easy! Eat, drink, and be merry!' But God said to him, 'You fool! You will die this very night. Then who will get everything you worked for?' Yes, a person is a fool to store up earthly wealth but not have a rich relationship with God.'" (NLT)

John 6:27-29 "Do not labor for the food which perishes, but for the food which endures to everlasting life, which the Son of Man will give you, because God the Father has set His seal on Him. Then they said to Him, 'What shall we do, that we may work the works of God?' Jesus answered and said to them, 'This is the work of God, that you believe in Him whom He sent.'" (NKJ)

John 9:4 "We must quickly carry out the tasks assigned us by the one who sent us. The night is coming, and then no one can work." (NLT)

John 10:37-38 "If I am not doing the works [performing the deeds] of My Father, then do not believe Me [do not adhere to Me and trust Me and rely on Me]. But if I do them, even though you do not believe Me or have faith in Me, [at least] believe the works and have faith in what I do, in order that you may know and understand [clearly] that the Father is in Me, and I am in the Father [One with Him]." (AMP)

John 14:12 "Most assuredly, I say to you, he who believes in Me, the works that I do he will do also; and greater *works* than these he will do, because I go to My Father." (NKJ)

GIVING & FINANCES

Matthew 6:1-4 "Take heed that you do not do your charitable deeds before men, to be seen by them. Otherwise you have no reward from your Father in heaven. Therefore, when you do a charitable deed, do not sound a trumpet before you as the hypocrites do in the synagogues and in the streets, that they may have glory from men. Assuredly, I say to you, they have their reward. But when you do a charitable deed, do not let your left hand know what your right hand is doing, that your charitable deed may be in secret; and your Father who sees in secret will Himself reward you openly." (NKJ)

Matthew 5:23-26 "So if when you are offering your gift at the altar you there remember that your brother has any [grievance] against you, leave your gift at the altar and go. First make peace with your brother, and then come back and present your gift. Come to terms quickly with your accuser while you are on the way traveling with him, lest your accuser hand you over to the judge, and the judge to the guard, and you be put in prison.

Truly I say to you, you will not be released until you have paid the last fraction of a penny." (AMP)

Mark 6:37 "But He replied to them, 'Give them something to eat yourselves.' And they said to Him, 'Shall we go and buy 200 denarii [about forty dollars] worth of bread and give it to them to eat?'" (AMP)

Mark 10:21 "Then Jesus, looking at him, loved him, and said to him, 'One thing you lack: Go your way, sell whatever you have and give to the poor, and you will have treasure in heaven; and come, take up the cross, and follow Me.'" (NKJ)

The Widow's Mite
(Mark)

Mark 12:41-44 "Jesus sat down near the collection box in the Temple and watched as the crowds dropped in their money. Many rich people put in large amounts. Then a poor widow came and dropped in two small coins. Jesus called his disciples to him and said, 'I tell you the truth, this poor widow has given more than all the others who are making contributions. For they gave a tiny part of their surplus, but she, poor as she is, has given everything she had to live on.'" (NLT)

Luke 6:38 "Give, and it will be given to you: good measure, pressed down, shaken together, and running over will be put into your bosom. For with the same measure that you use, it will be measured back to you." (NKJ)

Luke 12:33-34 "Sell what you possess and give donations to the poor; provide yourselves with purses and handbags that do not grow old, an unfailing and inexhaustible treasure in the heavens, where no thief comes near and no moth destroys. For where your treasure is, there will your heart be also." (AMP)

Parable of the Unjust Steward

Luke 16:1-13 "Jesus told this story to his disciples: There was a certain rich man who had a manager handling his affairs. One day a report came that the manager was wasting his employer's money. So the employer called him in and said, 'What's this I hear about you? Get your report in order, because you are going to be fired.' The manager thought to himself, 'Now what? My boss has fired me. I don't have the strength to dig ditches, and I'm too proud to beg. Ah, I know how to ensure that I'll have plenty of friends who will give me a home when I am fired.' So he invited each person who owed money to his employer to come and discuss the situation. He asked the first one, 'How much do you owe him?' The man replied, 'I owe him 800 gallons of olive oil.' So the manager told him, 'Take the bill and quickly change it to 400 gallons. 'And how much do you owe my employer?' he asked the next man. 'I owe him 1,000 bushels of wheat,' was the reply. 'Here,' the manager said, 'take the bill and change it to 800 bushels.' The rich man had to admire the dishonest rascal for being so shrewd. And it is true that the children of this world are more shrewd in dealing with the world around them than are the children of the light. Here's the lesson: Use your worldly resources to benefit others and make friends. Then, when your earthly possessions are gone, they will welcome you to an eternal home.

If you are faithful in little things, you will be faithful in large ones. But if you are dishonest in little things, you won't be honest with greater responsibilities. And if you are untrustworthy about worldly wealth, who will trust you with the true riches of heaven? And if you are not faithful with other people's things, why should you be trusted with things of your own? No one can serve two masters. For you will hate one and love the other; you will be devoted to one and despise the other. You cannot serve both God and money.'" (NLT)

Luke 20:22-25 "'Is it lawful for us to pay taxes to Caesar or not?' But He perceived their craftiness, and said to them, 'Why do you test Me? Show Me a denarius. Whose image and inscription does it have?' They answered and said, 'Caesar's.' And He said to them, 'Render therefore to Caesar the things that are Caesar's, and to God the things that are God's.'" (NKJ)

The Widow's Mite
(Luke)

Luke 21:1-4 "And He looked up and saw the rich putting their gifts into the treasury, and He saw also a certain poor widow putting in two mites. So He said, "Truly I say to you that this poor widow has put in more than all; for all these out of their abundance have put in offerings for God, but she out of her poverty put in all the livelihood that she had." (NKJ)

Luke 22:36 "'But now,' he said, 'take your money and a traveler's bag. And if you don't have a sword, sell your cloak and buy one!'" (NLT)

John 2:15-16 "Jesus made a whip from some ropes and chased them all out of the Temple. He drove out the sheep and cattle, scattered the money changers' coins over the floor, and turned over their tables. Then, going over to the people who sold doves, he told them, 'Get these things out of here. Stop turning my Father's house into a market-place!'" (NLT)

GOVERNMENTAL AUTHORITY

Matthew 22:17-21 "'Tell us, therefore, what do You think? Is it lawful to pay taxes to Caesar, or not?' But Jesus perceived their wickedness, and said, 'Why do you test Me, *you* hypocrites? Show Me the tax money.' So they brought Him a denarius. And He said to them, 'Whose image and inscription *is* this?' They said to Him, 'Caesar's.' And He said to them, 'Render therefore to Caesar the things that are Caesar's, and to God the things that are God's.'" (NKJ)

Mark 12:14-17 "And they came up and said to Him, 'Teacher, we know that You are sincere and what You profess to be, that You cannot lie, and that You have no personal bias for anyone; for You are not influenced by partiality and have no regard for anyone's external condition or position, but in [and on the basis of] truth You teach the way of God. Is it lawful (permissible and right) to give tribute (poll taxes) to Caesar or not?

Should we pay [them] or should we not pay [them]?' But knowing their hypocrisy, He asked them, 'Why do you put Me to the test? Bring Me a coin (a denarius), so I may see it.' And they brought [Him one]. Then He asked them, 'Whose image (picture) is this? And whose superscription (title)?' They said to Him, 'Caesar's.' Jesus said to them, 'Pay to Caesar the things that are Caesar's and to God the things that are God's.' And they stood marveling and greatly amazed at Him." (AMP)

JUSTICE

Luke 18:2-8a "He said, 'In a certain city there was a judge who neither reverenced and feared God nor respected or considered man. And there was a widow in that city who kept coming to him and saying, Protect and defend and give me justice against my adversary. And for a time he would not; but later he said to himself, 'Though I have neither reverence or fear for God nor respect or consideration for man, yet because this widow continues to bother me, I will defend and protect and avenge her, lest she give me intolerable annoyance and wear me out by her continual coming or at the last she come and rail on me or assault me or strangle me.' Then the Lord said, 'Listen to what the unjust judge says! And will not [our just] God defend and protect and avenge His elect (His chosen ones), who cry to Him day and night? Will He defer them and delay help on their behalf? I tell you, He will defend and protect and avenge them speedily...'" (AMP)

Luke 18:29-30 "Yes, Jesus replied, 'and I assure you that everyone who has given up house or wife or brothers or parents or children, for the sake of the Kingdom of God, will be repaid many times over in this life, and will have eternal life in the world to come.'" (NLT)

PROPHECY & WARNINGS

Matthew 7:15-20 "Beware of false prophets who come disguised as harmless sheep but are really vicious wolves. You can identify them by their fruit, that is, by the way they act. Can you pick grapes from thornbushes, or figs from thistles? A good tree produces good fruit, and a bad tree produces bad fruit. A good tree can't produce bad fruit, and a bad tree can't produce good fruit. So every tree that does not produce good fruit is chopped down and thrown into the fire. Yes, just as you can identify a tree by its fruit, so you can identify people by their actions." (NLT)

Matthew 10:26 "But don't be afraid of those who threaten you. For the time is coming when everything that is covered will be revealed, and all that is secret will be made known to all." (NLT)

Matthew 11:21-24 "What sorrow awaits you, Korazin and Bethsaida! For if the miracles I did in you had been done in wicked Tyre and Sidon, their people would have repented of their sins long ago, clothing themselves in burlap and throwing ashes on their heads to show their remorse. I tell you, Tyre and Sidon will be better off on judgment day than you. And you people of Capernaum, will you be honored in heaven? No, you will go down to the place of the dead. For if the miracles I did for you had been done in wicked Sodom, it would still be here today. I tell you, even Sodom will be better off on judgment day than you." (NLT)

Matthew 12:39-42 "But He replied to them, 'An evil and adulterous generation (a generation morally unfaithful to God) seeks and demands a sign; but no sign shall be given to it except the sign of the prophet Jonah. For even as Jonah was three days and three nights in the belly of the sea monster, so will the Son of Man be three days and three nights in the heart of the earth. The men of Nineveh will stand up at the judgment with this generation and condemn it; for they repented at the preaching of Jonah, and behold, someone more and greater than Jonah is here! The queen of the South will stand up at the judgment with this generation and condemn it; for she came from the ends of the earth to listen to the wisdom of Solomon, and behold, someone more and greater than Solomon is here.'" (AMP)

Matthew 16:2-4 "He replied to them, 'When it is evening you say, 'It will be fair weather, for the sky is red, and in the morning, it will be stormy today, for the sky is red and has a gloomy and threatening look.' You know how to interpret the appearance of the sky, but you cannot interpret the signs of the times. A wicked and morally unfaithful generation craves a sign, but no sign shall be given to it except the sign of the prophet Jonah.' Then He left them and went away." (AMP)

Matthew 16:6 "Then Jesus said to them, 'Take heed and beware of the leaven of the Pharisees and the Sadducees.'" (NKJ)

Matthew 16:28 "Assuredly, I say to you, there are some standing here who shall not taste death till they see the Son of Man coming in His kingdom." (NKJ)

Matthew 17:11-13 "Jesus replied, 'Elijah is indeed coming first to get everything ready. But I tell you, Elijah has already come, but he wasn't recognized, and they chose to abuse him. And in the same way they will also make the Son of Man suffer.' Then the disciples realized he was talking about John the Baptist." (NLT)

Matthew 17:22-23 "Now while they were staying in Galilee, Jesus said to them, 'The Son of Man is about to be betrayed into the hands of men, and they will kill Him, and the third day He will be raised up.' And they were exceedingly sorrowful." (NKJ)

Matthew 19:28-30 "Jesus replied, 'I assure you that when the world is made new and the Son of Man sits upon his glorious throne, you who have been my followers will also sit on twelve thrones, judging the twelve tribes of Israel. And everyone who has given up houses or brothers or sisters or father or mother or children or property, for my sake, will receive a hundred times as much in return and will inherit eternal life. But many who are the greatest now will be least important then, and those who seem least important now will be the greatest then.'" (NLT)

Matthew 20:18-19 "Behold, we are going up to Jerusalem, and the Son of Man will be handed over to the chief priests and scribes; and they will sentence Him to death And deliver Him over to the Gentiles to be mocked and whipped and crucified, and He will be raised [to life] on the third day." (AMP)

Matthew 20:20-23 "Then the mother of James and John, the sons of Zebedee, came to Jesus with her sons. She knelt respectfully to ask a favor. 'What is your request?' he asked. She replied, 'In your Kingdom, please let my two sons sit in places of honor next to you, one on your right and the other on your left.' But Jesus answered by saying to them, 'You don't know what you are asking! Are you able to drink from the bitter cup of suffering I am about to drink?' 'Oh yes,' they replied, 'we are able!' Jesus told them, 'You will indeed drink from my bitter cup. But I have no right to say who will sit on my right or my left. My Father has prepared those places for the ones he has chosen.'" (NLT)

Matthew 21:2-3 "'Go into the village over there,' he said. 'As soon as you enter it, you will see a donkey tied there, with its colt beside it. Untie them and bring them to me. If anyone asks what you are doing, just say, 'The Lord needs them,' and he will immediately let you take them.'" (NLT)

Parable of the Wicked Vinedressers
(Matthew)

Matthew 21:33-44 "Listen to another parable: There was a master of a house who planted a vineyard and put a hedge around it and dug a wine vat in it and built a watch-tower. Then he let it out [for rent] to tenants and went into another country. When the fruit season drew near, he sent his servants to the tenants to get his [share of the] fruit. But the tenants took his servants and beat one, killed another, and stoned another. Again he sent other servants, more than the first time, and they treated them the same way. Finally he sent his own son to them, saying, 'They will respect and give heed to my son.' But when the tenants saw the son, they said to themselves, 'This is the heir; come on, let us kill him and have his inheritance.' And they took him and threw him out of the vineyard and killed him. Now when the owner of the vineyard comes back, what will he do to those tenants? They said to Him, 'He will put those wretches to a miserable death and rent the vineyard to other tenants of such a character that they will give him the fruits promptly in their season.' Jesus asked them, 'Have you never read in the Scriptures: The very Stone which the builders rejected and threw away has become the Cornerstone; this is the Lord's doing, and it is marvelous in our eyes? I tell you, for this reason the kingdom of God will be taken away from you and given to a people who will produce the fruits of it. And whoever falls on this Stone will be broken to pieces, but he on whom It falls will be crushed to powder' [and It will winnow him, scattering him like dust]." (AMP)

Matthew 22:30-32 "For when the dead rise, they will neither marry nor be given in marriage. In this respect they will be like the angels in heaven. But now, as to whether there will be a resurrection of the dead—haven't you ever read about this in the Scriptures? Long after Abraham, Isaac, and Jacob had died, God said, 'I am the God of Abraham, the God of Isaac, and the God of Jacob.' So he is the God of the living, not the dead." (NLT)

Matthew 23:37-39 "O Jerusalem, Jerusalem, the one who kills the prophets and stones those who are sent to her! How often I wanted to gather your children together, as a hen gathers her chicks under *her* wings, but you were not willing! See! Your house is left to you desolate; for I say to you, you shall see Me no more till you say, *'Blessed is He who comes in the name of the LORD!'"* (NKJ)

Tribulation of the End Time

Matthew 24:4-44 "And Jesus answered and said to them: Take heed that no one deceives you. For many will come in My name, saying, 'I am the Christ,' and will deceive many. And you will hear of wars and rumors of wars. See that you are not troubled; for all *these things* must come to pass, but the end is not yet. For nation will rise against nation, and kingdom against kingdom. And there will be famines, pestilences, and earthquakes in various places. All these *are* the beginning of sorrows. Then they will deliver you up to tribulation and kill you, and you will be hated by all nations for My name's sake. And then many will be offended, will betray one another, and will hate one another. Then many false prophets will rise up and deceive many. And because lawlessness will abound, the love of many will grow cold. But he who endures to the end shall be saved. And this gospel of the kingdom will be preached in all the world as a witness to all the nations, and then the end will come.

The Great Tribulation

Therefore when you see the *'abomination of desolation,'* spoken of by Daniel the prophet, standing in the holy place" (whoever reads, let him understand), then let those who are in Judea flee to the mountains. Let him who is on the housetop not go down to take anything out of his house. And let him who is in the field not go back to get his clothes. But woe to those who are pregnant and to those who are nursing babies in those days! And pray that your flight may not be in winter or on the Sabbath. For then there will be great tribulation, such as has not been since the beginning of the world until this time, no, nor ever shall be. And unless those days were shortened, no flesh would be saved; but for the elect's sake those days will be shortened. Then if anyone says to you, 'Look, here *is* the Christ!' or 'There!' do not believe *it*. For false christs and false prophets will rise and show great signs and wonders to deceive, if possible, even the elect. See, I have told you beforehand. Therefore if they say to you, 'Look, He is in the desert!' do not go out; or 'Look, *He is* in the inner rooms!' do not believe *it*. For as the lightning comes from the east and flashes to the west, so also will the coming of the Son of Man be. For wherever the carcass is, there the eagles will be gathered together.

The Coming of the Son of Man

Immediately after the tribulation of those days the sun will be darkened, and the moon will not give its light; the stars will fall from heaven, and the powers of the heavens will be shaken. Then the sign of the Son of Man will appear in heaven, and then all the tribes of the earth will mourn, and they will see the Son of Man coming on the clouds of heaven with power and great glory. And He will send His angels with a great sound of a trumpet, and they will gather together His elect from the four winds, from one end of heaven to the other.

Parable of the Fig Tree
(Matthew)

Now learn this parable from the fig tree: When its branch has already become tender and puts forth leaves, you know that summer *is* near. So you also, when you see all these things, know that it is near—at the doors! Assuredly, I say to you, this generation will by no means pass away till all these things take place. Heaven and earth will pass away, but My words will by no means pass away.

No One Knows the Day or Hour

But of that day and hour no one knows, not even the angels of heaven, but My Father only. But as the days of Noah *were,* so also will the coming of the Son of Man be. For as in the days before the flood, they were eating and drinking, marrying and giving in marriage, until the day that Noah entered the ark, and did not know until the flood came and took them all away, so also will the coming of the Son of Man be. Then two *men* will be in the field: one will be taken and the other left. Two *women will be* grinding at the mill: one will be taken and the other left. Watch therefore, for you do not know what hour your Lord is coming. But know this, that if the master of the house had known what hour the thief would come, he would have watched and not allowed his house to be broken into. Therefore you also be ready, for the Son of Man is coming at an hour you do not expect." (NKJ)

Matthew 26:2 "You know that after two days is the Passover, and the Son of Man will be delivered up to be crucified." (NKJ)

Matthew 26:32 "But after I am raised up [to life again], I will go ahead of you to Galilee." (AMP)

Mark 9:1 "And He said to them, 'Assuredly, I say to you that there are some standing here who will not taste death till they see the kingdom of God present with power.'" (NKJ)

Mark 9:11-13 "Then they asked him, 'Why do the teachers of religious law insist that Elijah must return before the Messiah comes?' Jesus responded, 'Elijah is indeed coming first to get everything ready. Yet why do the Scriptures say that the Son of Man must suffer greatly and be treated with utter contempt? But I tell you, Elijah has already come, and they chose to abuse him, just as the Scriptures predicted.'" (NLT)

Mark 9:31 "For He wanted to spend more time with his disciples and teach them. He said to them, 'The Son of Man is going to be betrayed into the hands of his enemies. He will be killed, but three days later he will rise from the dead.'" (NLT)

Mark 10:31 "But many who are the greatest now will be least important then, and those who seem least important now will be the greatest then." (NLT)

Mark 10:33-34 "Behold, we are going up to Jerusalem, and the Son of Man will be betrayed to the chief priests and to the scribes; and they will condemn Him to death and deliver Him to the Gentiles; and they will mock Him, and scourge Him, and spit on Him, and kill Him. And the third day He will rise again." (NKJ)

Mark 10:37-40 "They replied, 'When you sit on your glorious throne, we want to sit in places of honor next to you, one on your right and the other on your left.' But Jesus said to them, 'You don't know what you are asking! Are you able to drink from the bitter cup of suffering I am about to drink? Are you able to be baptized with the baptism of suffering I must be baptized with?' 'Oh yes,' they replied, 'we are able!' Then Jesus told them, 'You will indeed drink from my bitter cup and be baptized with my baptism of suffering. But I have no right to say who will sit on my right or my left. God has prepared those places for the ones he has chosen.'" (NLT)

Parable of the Wicked Vinedressers
(Mark)

Mark 12:1-11 "Then He began to speak to them in parables: A man planted a vineyard and set a hedge around *it,* dug *a place for* the wine vat and built a tower. And he leased it to vinedressers and went into a far country. Now at vintage-time he sent a servant to the vinedressers, that he might receive some of the fruit of the vineyard from the vinedressers. And they took *him* and beat him and sent *him* away empty-handed. Again he sent them another servant, and at him they threw stones, wounded *him* in the head, and sent *him* away shamefully treated. And again he sent another, and him they killed; and many others, beating some and killing some. Therefore still having one son, his beloved, he also sent him to them last, saying, 'They will respect my son.' But those vinedressers said among themselves, 'This is the heir. Come, let us kill him, and the inheritance will be ours.' So they took him and killed *him* and cast *him* out of the vineyard. Therefore what will the owner of the vineyard do? He will come and destroy the vinedressers, and give the vineyard to others. Have you not even read this scripture:

'The stone which the builders rejected
Has become the chief cornerstone.
This was the LORD's doing,
And it is marvelous in our eyes'?" (NKJ)

Mark 13:5-23 "Jesus replied, 'Don't let anyone mislead you, for many will come in my name, claiming, 'I am the Messiah.' They will deceive many. And you will hear of wars and threats of wars, but don't panic. Yes, these things must take place, but the end won't follow immediately. Nation will go to war against nation, and kingdom against kingdom. There will be earthquakes in many parts of the world, as well as famines. But this is only the first of the birth pains, with more to come. When these things begin to happen, watch out! You will be handed over to the local councils and beaten in the synagogues. You will stand trial before governors and kings because you are my followers. But this will be your opportunity to tell them about me. For the Good News must first be preached to all nations. But when you are arrested and stand trial, don't worry in advance about what to say. Just say what God tells you at that time, for it is not you who will be speaking, but the Holy Spirit. A brother will betray his brother to death, a father will betray his own child, and children will rebel against their parents and cause them to be killed. And everyone will hate you because you are my followers. But the one who endures to the end will be saved. The day is coming when you will see the sacrilegious object that causes desecration standing where he should not be." (Reader, pay attention!) "Then those in Judea must flee to the hills. A person out on the deck of a roof must not go down into the house to pack. A person out in the field must not return even to get a coat. How terrible it will be for pregnant women and for nursing mothers in those days. And pray that your flight will not be in winter. For there will be greater anguish in those days than at any time since God created the world. And it will never be so great again.

In fact, unless the Lord shortens that time of calamity, not a single person will survive. But for the sake of his chosen ones he has shortened those days. Then if anyone tells you, 'Look, here is the Messiah,' or 'There he is,' don't believe it. For false messiahs and false prophets will rise up and perform signs and wonders so as to deceive, if possible, even God's chosen ones. Watch out! I have warned you about this ahead of time!'" (NLT)

Parable of the Fig Tree
(Mark)

Mark 13:28-31 "Now learn a lesson from the fig tree: as soon as its branch becomes tender and it puts forth its leaves, you recognize and know that summer is near.

So also, when you see these things happening, you may recognize and know that He is near, at [the very] door. Surely I say to you, this generation (the whole multitude of people living at that one time) positively will not perish or pass away before all these things take place. Heaven and earth will perish and pass away, but My words will not perish or pass away." (AMP)

Mark 13:32-37 "But of that day and hour no one knows, not even the angels in heaven, nor the Son, but only the Father. Take heed, watch and pray; for you do not know when the time is. *It is* like a man going to a far country, who left his house and gave authority to his servants, and to each his work, and commanded the doorkeeper to watch. Watch therefore, for you do not know when the master of the house is coming—in the evening, at midnight, at the crowing of the rooster, or in the morning— lest, coming suddenly, he find you sleeping. And what I say to you, I say to all: Watch!" (NKJ)

Mark 14:13-21 "So Jesus sent two of them into Jerusalem with these instructions: 'As you go into the city, a man carrying a pitcher of water will meet you. Follow him. At the house he enters, say to the owner, 'The Teacher asks: Where is the guest room where I can eat the Passover meal with my disciples?' He will take you upstairs to a large room that is already set up. That is where you should prepare our meal.' So the two disciples went into the city and found everything just as Jesus had said, and they prepared the Passover meal there. In the evening Jesus arrived with the twelve disciples. As they were at the table eating, Jesus said, 'I tell you the truth, one of you eating with me here will betray me.' Greatly distressed, each one asked in turn, 'Am I the one?' He replied, 'It is one of you twelve who is eating from this bowl with me. For the Son of Man must die, as the Scriptures declared long ago. But how terrible it will be for the one who betrays him. It would be far better for that man if he had never been born!'" (NLT)

Mark 14:25, 28 "Solemnly and surely I tell you, I shall not again drink of the fruit of the vine till that day when I drink it of a new and a higher quality in God's kingdom...But after I am raised [to life], I will go before you into Galilee." (AMP)

Luke 9:22 "'The Son of Man must suffer many terrible things,' he said. 'He will be rejected by the elders, the leading priests, and the teachers of religious law. He will be killed, but on the third day he will be raised from the dead.'" (NLT)

Luke 9:44 "Let these words sink down into your ears, for the Son of Man is about to be betrayed into the hands of men." (NKJ)

Luke 11:29-32 "And while the crowds were thickly gathered together, He began to say, 'This is an evil generation. It seeks a sign, and no sign will be given to it except the sign of Jonah the prophet. For as Jonah became a sign to the Ninevites, so also the Son of Man will be to this generation.

The queen of the South will rise up in the judgment with the men of this generation and condemn them, for she came from the ends of the earth to hear the wisdom of Solomon; and indeed a greater than Solomon *is* here. The men of Nineveh will rise up in the judgment with this generation and condemn it, for they repented at the preaching of Jonah; and indeed a greater than Jonah *is* here.'" (NKJ)

Luke 12:1-3 "Meanwhile, the crowds grew until thousands were milling about and stepping on each other. Jesus turned first to his disciples and warned them, 'Beware of the yeast of the Pharisees—their hypocrisy. The time is coming when everything that is covered up will be revealed, and all that is secret will be made known to all. Whatever you have said in the dark will be heard in the light, and what you have whispered behind closed doors will be shouted from the housetops for all to hear!'" (NLT)

Luke 17:22-36 "Then He said to the disciples, 'The days will come when you will desire to see one of the days of the Son of Man, and you will not see *it.* And they will say to you, 'Look here!' or 'Look there!' Do not go after *them* or follow *them.* For as the lightning that flashes out of one *part* under heaven shines to the other *part* under heaven, so also the Son of Man will be in His day. But first He must suffer many things and be rejected by this generation. And as it was in the days of Noah, so it will be also in the days of the Son of Man: They ate, they drank, they married wives, they were given in marriage, until the day that Noah entered the ark, and the flood came and destroyed them all. Likewise as it was also in the days of Lot: They ate, they drank, they bought, they sold, they planted, they built; but on the day that Lot went out of Sodom it rained fire and brimstone from heaven and destroyed *them* all. Even so will it be in the day when the Son of Man is revealed. In that day, he who is on the housetop, and his goods *are* in the house, let him not come down to take them away. And likewise the one who is in the field, let him not turn back. Remember Lot's wife. Whoever seeks to save his life will lose it, and whoever loses his life will preserve it. I tell you, in that night there will be two *men* in one bed: the one will be taken and the other will be left. Two *women* will be grinding together: the one will be taken and the other left. Two *men* will be in the field: the one will be taken and the other left.'" (NKJ)

Luke 18:31-33 "Then He took the twelve aside and said to them, 'Behold, we are going up to Jerusalem, and all things that are written by the prophets concerning the Son of Man will be accomplished. For He will be delivered to the Gentiles and will be mocked and insulted and spit upon. They will scourge *Him* and kill Him. And the third day He will rise again.'" (NKJ)

Luke 19:29-32 "As he came to the towns of Bethphage and Bethany on the Mount of Olives, he sent two disciples ahead. 'Go into that village over there,' he told them. 'As you enter it, you will see a young donkey tied there that no one has ever ridden. Untie it and bring it here. If anyone asks, 'Why are you untying that colt?' just say, 'The Lord needs it.' So they went and found the colt, just as Jesus had said." (NLT)

Luke 19:41-44 "Now as He drew near, He saw the city and wept over it, saying, 'If you had known, even you, especially in this your day, the things *that make* for your peace! But now they are hidden from your eyes. For days will come upon you when your enemies will build an embankment around you, surround you and close you in on every side, and level you, and your children within you, to the ground; and they will not leave in you one stone upon another, because you did not know the time of your visitation.'" (NKJ)

Parable of the Wicked Vinedressers
(Luke)

Luke 20:9-18 "Then He began to tell the people this parable: A certain man planted a vineyard, leased it to vinedressers, and went into a far country for a long time. Now at vintage-time he sent a servant to the vinedressers, that they might give him some of the fruit of the vineyard. But the vinedressers beat him and sent *him* away empty-handed. Again he sent another servant; and they beat him also, treated *him* shamefully, and sent *him* away empty-handed. And again he sent a third; and they wounded him also and cast *him* out. Then the owner of the vineyard said, 'What shall I do? I will send my beloved son. Probably they will respect *him* when they see him.' But when the vinedressers saw him, they reasoned among themselves, saying, 'This is the heir. Come, let us kill him, that the inheritance may be ours.' So they cast him out of the vineyard and killed *him*. Therefore what will the owner of the vineyard do to them? He will come and destroy those vinedressers and give the vineyard to others. And when they heard *it* they said, 'Certainly not!' Then He looked at them and said, 'What then is this that is written:

'The stone which the builders rejected
Has become the chief cornerstone'?

Whoever falls on that stone will be broken; but on whomever it falls, it will grind him to powder.'" (NKJ)

Luke 21:8-11 "And He said, 'Be on your guard and be careful that you are not led astray; for many will come in My name [appropriating to themselves the name Messiah which belongs to Me], saying, 'I am He!' and, 'The time is at hand!' Do not go out after them.

And when you hear of wars and insurrections (disturbances, disorder, and confusion), do not become alarmed and panic-stricken and terrified; for all this must take place first, but the end will not [come] immediately.' Then He told them, 'Nation will rise against nation, and kingdom against kingdom. There will be mighty and violent earthquakes, and in various places famines and pestilences (plagues: malignant and contagious or infectious epidemic diseases which are deadly and devastating); and there will be sights of terror and great signs from heaven.'" (AMP)

Luke 21:20-24 "And when you see Jerusalem surrounded by armies, then you will know that the time of its destruction has arrived. Then those in Judea must flee to the hills. Those in Jerusalem must get out, and those out in the country should not return to the city. For those will be days of God's vengeance, and the prophetic words of the Scriptures will be fulfilled. How terrible it will be for pregnant women and for nursing mothers in those days. For there will be disaster in the land and great anger against this people. They will be killed by the sword or sent away as captives to all the nations of the world. And Jerusalem will be trampled down by the Gentiles until the period of the Gentiles comes to an end." (NLT)

Parable of the Fig Tree
(Luke)

Luke 21:29-33 "Then He spoke to them a parable: Look at the fig tree, and all the trees. When they are already budding, you see and know for yourselves that summer is now near. So you also, when you see these things happening, know that the kingdom of God is near. Assuredly, I say to you, this generation will by no means pass away till all things take place. Heaven and earth will pass away, but My words will by no means pass away." (NKJ)

Luke 22:9-13 "So they said to Him, 'Where do You want us to prepare?' And He said to them, 'Behold, when you have entered the city, a man will meet you carrying a pitcher of water; follow him into the house which he enters. Then you shall say to the master of the house, 'The Teacher says to you, 'Where is the guest room where I may eat the Passover with My disciples?' Then he will show you a large, furnished upper room; there make ready.' So they went and found it just as He had said to them, and they prepared the Passover." (NKJ)

Luke 22:15-18 "And He said to them, 'I have earnestly and intensely desired to eat this Passover with you before I suffer; For I say to you, I shall eat it no more until it is fulfilled in the kingdom of God.' And He took a cup, and when He had given thanks, He said, 'Take this and divide and distribute it among yourselves; For I say to you that from now on I shall not drink of the fruit of the vine at all until the kingdom of God comes.'" (AMP)

Luke 22:37 "For the time has come for this prophecy about me to be fulfilled: 'He was counted among the rebels.' Yes, everything written about me by the prophets will come true." (NLT)

Luke 24:44 "Then He said to them, 'This is what I told you while I was still with you: everything which is written concerning Me in the Law of Moses and the Prophets and the Psalms must be fulfilled.'" (AMP)

John 1:48-51 "Nathanael said to Jesus, 'How do You know me?' [How is it that You know these things about me?] Jesus answered him, 'Before [ever] Philip called you, when you were still under the fig tree, I saw you.' Nathanael answered, 'Teacher, You are the Son of God! You are the King of Israel!' Jesus replied, 'Because I said to you, 'I saw you beneath the fig tree', do you believe in and rely on and trust in Me? You shall see greater things than this!' Then He said to him, 'I assure you, most solemnly I tell you all, you shall see heaven opened, and the angels of God ascending and descending upon the Son of Man!'" (AMP)

John 2:19 "Jesus answered and said to them, 'Destroy this temple, and in three days I will raise it up.'" (NKJ)

John 7:5-8 "For even His brothers did not believe in Him. Then Jesus said to them, 'My time has not yet come, but your time is always ready. The world cannot hate you, but it hates Me because I testify of it that its works are evil. You go up to this feast. I am not yet going up to this feast, for My time has not yet fully come.'" (NKJ)

John 7:33-34 "But Jesus told them, 'I will be with you only a little longer. Then I will return to the one who sent me. You will search for me but not find me. And you cannot go where I am going.'" (NLT)

John 8:21 "Therefore He said again to them, I am going away, and you will be looking for Me, and you will die in (under the curse of) your sin. Where I am going, it is not possible for you to come." (AMP)

John 12:32 "And I, if and when I am lifted up from the earth [on the cross], will draw and attract all men [Gentiles as well as Jews] to Myself." (AMP)

John 14:19-20 "A little while longer and the world will see Me no more, but you will see Me. Because I live, you will live also. At that day you will know that I *am* in My Father, and you in Me, and I in you." (NKJ)

John 14:28-30 "You heard Me tell you, I am going away and I am coming [back] to you. If you [really] loved Me, you would have been glad, because I am going to the Father; for the Father is greater and mightier than I am. And now I have told you [this] before it occurs, so that when it does take place you may believe and have faith in and rely on Me.

I will not talk with you much more, for the prince (evil genius, ruler) of the world is coming. And he has no claim on Me. [He has nothing in common with Me; there is nothing in Me that belongs to him, and he has no power over Me.]" (AMP)

John 16:2-4 "They will put you out of the synagogues; yes, the time is coming that whoever kills you will think that he offers God service. And these things they will do to you because they have not known the Father nor Me. But these things I have told you, that when the time comes, you may remember that I told you of them. And these things I did not say to you at the beginning, because I was with you." (NKJ)

John 16:19-22 "Jesus realized they wanted to ask him about it, so he said, 'Are you asking yourselves what I meant? I said in a little while you won't see me, but a little while after that you will see me again. I tell you the truth, you will weep and mourn over what is going to happen to me, but the world will rejoice. You will grieve, but your grief will suddenly turn to wonderful joy. It will be like a woman suffering the pains of labor. When her child is born, her anguish gives way to joy because she has brought a new baby into the world. So you have sorrow now, but I will see you again; then you will rejoice, and no one can rob you of that joy.'" (NLT)

RELATIONSHIPS & CONFLICT RESOLUTION

Matthew 5:38-42 "You have heard that it was said, 'An eye for an eye, and a tooth for a tooth.' But I say to you, do not resist the evil man [who injures you]; but if anyone strikes you on the right jaw or cheek, turn to him the other one too. And if anyone wants to sue you and take your undershirt (tunic), let him have your coat also. And if anyone forces you to go one mile, go with him two [miles]. Give to him who keeps on begging from you, and do not turn away from him who would borrow [at interest] from you." (AMP)

Matthew 7:6 "Do not give what is holy to the dogs; nor cast your pearls before swine, lest they trample them under their feet, and turn and tear you in pieces." (NKJ)

Matthew 7:9-12 "Or what man is there among you who, if his son asks for bread, will give him a stone? Or if he asks for a fish, will he give him a serpent? If you then, being evil, know how to give good gifts to your children, how much more will your Father who is in heaven give good things to those who ask Him! Therefore, whatever you want men to do to you, do also to them, for this is the Law and the Prophets." (NKJ)

Matthew 10:24 "A disciple is not above *his* teacher, nor a servant above his master." (NKJ)

Matthew 13:57 "So they were offended at Him. But Jesus said to them, 'A prophet is not without honor except in his own country and in his own house.'" (NKJ)

Matthew 16:13-15 "When Jesus came into the region of Caesarea Philippi, He asked His disciples, saying, 'Who do men say that I, the Son of Man, am?' So they said, 'Some *say* John the Baptist, some Elijah, and others Jeremiah or one of the prophets.' He said to them, 'But who do you say that I am?'" (NKJ)

Matthew 18:7-9 "What sorrow awaits the world, because it tempts people to sin. Temptations are inevitable, but what sorrow awaits the person who does the tempting. So if your hand or foot causes you to sin, cut it off and throw it away. It's better to enter eternal life with only one hand or one foot than to be thrown into eternal fire with both of your hands and feet. And if your eye causes you to sin, gouge it out and throw it away. It's better to enter eternal life with only one eye than to have two eyes and be thrown into the fire of hell." (NLT)

Matthew 18:15-17 "If your brother wrongs you, go and show him his fault, between you and him privately. If he listens to you, you have won back your brother. But if he does not listen, take along with you one or two others, so that every word may be confirmed and upheld by the testimony of two or three witnesses. If he pays no attention to them [refusing to listen and obey], tell it to the church; and if he refuses to listen even to the church, let him be to you as a pagan and a tax collector." (AMP)

Mark 6:4 "Then Jesus told them, 'A prophet is honored everywhere except in his own hometown and among his relatives and his own family.'" (NLT)

Mark 8:27-29 "Now Jesus and His disciples went out to the towns of Caesarea Philippi; and on the road He asked His disciples, saying to them, 'Who do men say that I am?' So they answered, 'John the Baptist; but some *say,* Elijah; and others, one of the prophets.' He said to them, 'But who do you say that I am?' Peter answered and said to Him, 'You are the Christ.'" (NKJ)

Mark 9:35 "And He sat down, called the twelve, and said to them, 'If anyone desires to be first, he shall be last of all and servant of all.'" (NKJ)

Mark 9:39-40 "But Jesus said, 'Do not restrain or hinder or forbid him; for no one who does a mighty work in My name will soon afterward be able to speak evil of Me.

For he who is not against us is for us." (AMP)

Mark 9:49-50 "For everyone will be tested with fire. Salt is good for seasoning. But if it loses its flavor, how do you make it salty again? You must have the qualities of salt among yourselves and live in peace with each other." (NLT)

Mark 10:19 "You know the commandments: *'Do not commit adultery,' 'Do not murder,' 'Do not steal,' 'Do not bear false witness,' 'Do not defraud,' 'Honor your father and your mother.'"* (NKJ)

Mark 10:42-45 "But Jesus called them to [Him] and said to them, 'You know that those who are recognized as governing and are supposed to rule the Gentiles (the nations) lord it over them [ruling with absolute power, holding them in subjection], and their great men exercise authority and dominion over them. But this is not to be so among you; instead, whoever desires to be great among you must be your servant, and whoever wishes to be most important and first in rank among you must be slave of all. For even the Son of Man came not to have service rendered to Him, but to serve, and to give His life as a ransom for (instead of) many.'" (AMP)

Luke 6:27-37 "But to you who are willing to listen, I say, love your enemies! Do good to those who hate you. Bless those who curse you. Pray for those who hurt you. If someone slaps you on one cheek, offer the other cheek also. If someone demands your coat, offer your shirt also. Give to anyone who asks; and when things are taken away from you, don't try to get them back. Do to others as you would like them to do to you.

If you love only those who love you, why should you get credit for that? Even sinners love those who love them! And if you do good only to those who do good to you, why should you get credit? Even sinners do that much! And if you lend money only to those who can repay you, why should you get credit? Even sinners will lend to other sinners for a full return. Love your enemies! Do good to them. Lend to them without expecting to be repaid. Then your reward from heaven will be very great, and you will truly be acting as children of the Most High, for he is kind to those who are unthankful and wicked. You must be compassionate, just as your Father is compassionate. Do not judge others, and you will not be judged. Do not condemn others, or it will all come back against you. Forgive others, and you will be forgiven." (NLT)

Luke 6:41-42 "And why do you look at the speck in your brother's eye, but do not perceive the plank in your own eye? Or how can you say to your brother, 'Brother, let me remove the speck that *is* in your eye,' when you yourself do not see the plank that *is* in your own eye? Hypocrite! First remove the plank from your own eye, and then you will see clearly to remove the speck that is in your brother's eye." (NKJ)

Luke 10:16 "He who hears you hears Me, he who rejects you rejects Me, and he who rejects Me rejects Him who sent Me." (NKJ)

Parable of the Good Samaritan

Luke 10:30-37 "Then Jesus answered and said: A certain *man* went down from Jerusalem to Jericho, and fell among thieves, who stripped him of his clothing, wounded *him,* and departed, leaving *him* half dead. Now by chance a certain priest came down that road. And when he saw him, he passed by on the other side. Likewise a Levite, when he arrived at the place, came and looked, and passed by on the other side. But a certain Samaritan, as he jour- neyed, came where he was. And when he saw him, he had compassion. So he went to *him* and bandaged his wounds, pouring on oil and wine; and he set him on his own animal, brought him to an inn, and took care of him. On the next day, when he departed, he took out two denarii, gave *them* to the innkeeper, and said to him, 'Take care of him; and whatever more you spend, when I come again, I will repay you.' So which of these three do you think was neighbor to him who fell among the thieves?' And he said, 'He who showed mercy on him.' Then Jesus said to him, 'Go and do likewise.'" (NKJ)

Luke 12:57-59 "Why can't you decide for yourselves what is right? When you are on the way to court with your accuser, try to settle the matter before you get there. Otherwise, your accuser may drag you before the judge, who will hand you over to an officer, who will throw you into prison. And if that happens, you won't be free again until you have paid the very last penny." (NLT)

Luke 14:8-14 "When you are invited to a wedding feast, don't sit in the seat of honor. What if someone who is more distinguished than you has also been invited? The host will come and say, 'Give this person your seat.' Then you will be embarrassed, and you will have to take whatever seat is left at the foot of the table! Instead, take the lowest place at the foot of the table. Then when your host sees you, he will come and say, 'Friend, we have a better place for you!' Then you will be honored in front of all the other guests. For those who exalt themselves will be humbled, and those who humble themselves will be exalted.' Then he turned to his host. 'When you put on a luncheon or a banquet,' he said, 'don't invite your friends, brothers, relatives, and rich neighbors. For they will invite you back, and that will be your only reward. Instead, invite the poor, the crippled, the lame, and the blind. Then at the resurrection of the righteous, God will reward you for inviting those who could not repay you.'" (NLT)

Luke 17:1-4 "And [Jesus] said to His disciples, 'Temptations (snares, traps set to entice to sin) are sure to come, but woe to him by or through whom they come! It would be more profitable for him if a millstone were hung around his neck and he were hurled into the sea than that he should cause to sin or be a snare to one of these little ones [lowly in rank or influence]. Pay attention and always be on your guard [looking out for one another]. If your brother sins (misses the mark), solemnly tell him so and reprove him, and if he repents (feels sorry for having sinned), forgive him. And even if he sins against you seven times in a day, and turns to you seven times and says, I repent [I am sorry], you must forgive him' (give up resentment and consider the offense as recalled and annulled)." (AMP)

Luke 21:16-19 "You will be betrayed even by parents and brothers, relatives and friends; and they will put *some* of you to death. And you will be hated by all for My name's sake. But not a hair of your head shall be lost. By your patience possess your souls." (NKJ)

Luke 22:26-27 "But not so *among* you; on the contrary, he who is greatest among you, let him be as the younger, and he who governs as he who serves. For who *is* greater, he who sits at the table, or he who serves? *Is* it not he who sits at the table? Yet I am among you as the One who serves." (NKJ)

John 13:13-17 "You call Me the Teacher (Master) and the Lord, and you are right in doing so, for that is what I am. If I then, your Lord and Teacher (Master), have washed your feet, you ought [it is your duty, you are under obligation, you owe it] to wash one another's feet. For I have given you this as an example, so that you should do [in your turn] what I have done to you. I assure you, most solemnly I tell you, a servant is not greater than his master, and no one who is sent is superior to the one who sent him.

If you know these things, blessed and happy and to be envied are you if you practice them [if you act accordingly and really do them]." (AMP)

John 13:20 "I tell you the truth, anyone who welcomes my messenger is welcoming me, and anyone who welcomes me is welcoming the Father who sent me." (NLT)

JESUS' RELATIONSHIP WITH THE FATHER

Matthew 11:27 "My Father has entrusted everything to me. No one truly knows the Son except the Father, and no one truly knows the Father except the Son and those to whom the Son chooses to reveal him." (NLT)

Matthew 26:38-39 "Then He said to them, 'My soul is very sad and deeply grieved, so that I am almost dying of sorrow. Stay here and keep awake and keep watch with Me.'

And going a little farther, He threw Himself upon the ground on His face and prayed saying, 'My Father, if it is possible, let this cup pass away from Me; nevertheless, not what I will [not what I desire], but as You will and desire.'" (AMP)

Matthew 26:42 "Again, a second time, He went away and prayed, saying, 'O My Father, if this cup cannot pass away from Me unless I drink it, Your will be done.'" (NKJ)

Matthew 26:53 "Or do you think that I cannot now pray to My Father, and He will provide Me with more than twelve legions of angels?" (NKJ)

Mark 14:36 "And He was saying, Abba, [which means] Father, everything is possible for You. Take away this cup from Me; yet not what I will, but what You [will]." (AMP)

Mark 15:32-34 "...Even those who were crucified with Him reviled Him. Now when the sixth hour had come, there was darkness over the whole land until the ninth hour. And at the ninth hour Jesus cried out with a loud voice, saying, 'Eloi, Eloi, lama sabachthani?' which is translated, *'My God, My God, why have You forsaken Me?'*" (NKJ)

Luke 2:49 "And He said to them, 'Why did you seek Me? Did you not know that I must be about My Father's business?'" (NKJ)

Luke 4:18-19 "The Spirit of the Lord [is] upon Me, because He has anointed Me [the Anointed One, the Messiah] to preach the good news (the Gospel) to the poor; He has sent Me to announce release to the captives and recovery of sight to the blind, to send forth as delivered those who are oppressed [who are downtrodden, bruised, crushed, and broken down by calamity], to proclaim the accepted and acceptable year of the Lord [the day when salvation and the free favors of God profusely abound." (AMP)

Luke 10:21-22 "In that same hour He rejoiced and gloried in the Holy Spirit and said, 'I thank You, Father, Lord of heaven and earth, that You have concealed these things [relating to salvation] from the wise and understanding and learned, and revealed them to babes (the childish, unskilled, and untaught). Yes, Father, for such was Your gracious will and choice and good pleasure. All things have been given over into My power by My Father; and no one knows Who the Son is except the Father, or Who the Father is except the Son and anyone to whom the Son may choose to reveal and make Him known.'" (AMP)

Prayer in the Garden

Luke 22:41-42 "And He was withdrawn from them about a stone's throw, and He knelt down and prayed, saying, 'Father, if it is Your will, take this cup away from Me; nevertheless not My will, but Yours, be done.'" (NKJ)

Luke 23:33-34a "And when they had come to the place called Calvary, there they crucified Him, and the criminals, one on the right hand and the other on the left. Then Jesus said, 'Father, forgive them, for they do not know what they do.'" (NKJ)

Luke 23:46 "And when Jesus had cried out with a loud voice, He said, 'Father, *into Your hands I commit My spirit.'* Having said this, He breathed His last." (NKJ)

John 5:19-23 "So Jesus answered them by saying, 'I assure you, most solemnly I tell you, the Son is able to do nothing of Himself (of His own accord); but He is able to do only what He sees the Father doing, for whatever the Father does is what the Son does in the same way [in His turn]. The Father dearly loves the Son and discloses to (shows) Him everything that He Himself does. And He will disclose to Him (let Him see) greater things yet than these, so that you may marvel and be full of wonder and astonishment.

Just as the Father raises up the dead and gives them life [makes them live on], even so the Son also gives life to whomever He wills and is pleased to give it. Even the Father judges no one, for He has given all judgment (the last judgment and the whole business of judging) entirely into the hands of the Son, so that all men may give honor (reverence, homage) to the Son just as they give honor to the Father. [In fact] whoever does not honor the Son does not honor the Father, who has sent Him.'" (AMP)

John 5:26-27,30 "For as the Father has life in Himself, so He has granted the Son to have life in Himself, and has given Him authority to execute judgment also, because He is the Son of Man... I can of Myself do nothing. As I hear, I judge; and My judgment is righteous, because I do not seek My own will but the will of the Father who sent Me." (NKJ)

John 6:38-39 "For I have come down from heaven not to do My own will and purpose but to do the will and purpose of Him Who sent Me. And this is the will of Him Who sent Me, that I should not lose any of all that He has given Me, but that I should give new life and raise [them all] up at the last day." (AMP)

John 7:16-17 "Jesus answered them by saying, My teaching is not My own, but His Who sent Me. If any man desires to do His will (God's pleasure), he will know (have the needed illumination to recognize, and can tell for himself) whether the teaching is from God or whether I am speaking from Myself and of My own accord and on My own authority." (AMP)

John 7:28-29 "Then Jesus cried out, as He taught in the temple, saying, 'You both know Me, and you know where I am from; and I have not come of Myself, but He who sent Me is true, whom you do not know. But I know Him, for I am from Him, and He sent Me.'" (NKJ)

John 8:16-18 "Yet even if I do judge, My judgment is true [My decision is right]; for I am not alone [in making it], but [there are two of Us] I and the Father, who sent Me.

In your [own] Law it is written that the testimony (evidence) of two persons is reliable and valid. I am One [of the Two] bearing testimony concerning Myself; and My Father, who sent Me, He also testifies about Me." (AMP)

John 8:26,28-29 "'I have many things to say and to judge concerning you, but He who sent Me is true; and I speak to the world those things which I heard from Him'...Then Jesus said to them, 'When you lift up the Son of Man, then you will know that I am *He,* and *that* I do nothing of Myself; but as My Father taught Me, I speak these things. And He who sent Me is with Me. The Father has not left Me alone, for I always do those things that please Him.'" (NKJ)

John 10:17-18 "Therefore My Father loves Me, because I lay down My life that I may take it again. No one takes it from Me, but I lay it down of Myself. I have power to lay it down, and I have power to take it again. This command I have received from My Father." (NKJ)

John 10:30 "The Father and I are one." (NLT)

John 11:41b-42 "...And Jesus lifted up His eyes and said, 'Father, I thank You that You have heard Me. Yes, I know You always hear and listen to Me, but I have said this on account 'of and for the benefit of the people standing around, so that they may believe that You did send Me [that You have made Me Your Messenger].'" (AMP)

John 12:49-50 "This is because I have never spoken on My own authority or of My own accord or as self-appointed, but the Father Who sent Me has Himself given Me orders [concerning] what to say and what to tell. And I know that His commandment is (means) eternal life. So whatever I speak, I am saying [exactly] what My Father has told Me to say and in accordance with His instructions." (AMP)

John 13:31-32 "So, when he had gone out, Jesus said, 'Now the Son of Man is glorified, and God is glorified in Him. If God is glorified in Him, God will also glorify Him in Himself, and glorify Him immediately.'" (NKJ)

John 14:7-11 "If you had known Me [had learned to recognize Me], you would also have known My Father. From now on, you know Him and have seen Him.' Philip said to Him, 'Lord, show us the Father [cause us to see the Father—that is all we ask]; then we shall be satisfied.' Jesus replied, 'Have I been with all of you for so long a time, and do you not recognize and know Me yet, Philip? Anyone who has seen Me has seen the Father. How can you say then, Show us the Father? Do you not believe that I am in the Father, and that the Father is in Me? What I am telling you I do not say on My own authority and of My own accord; but the Father Who lives continually in Me does the (His) works (His own miracles, deeds of power). Believe Me that I am in the Father and the Father in Me; or else believe Me for the sake of the [very] works themselves. [If you cannot trust Me, at least let these works that I do in My Father's name convince you.]'" (AMP)

John 14:31 "But I will do what the Father requires of me, so that the world will know that I love the Father. Come, let's be going." (NLT)

John 16:28 "I came forth from the Father and have come into the world. Again, I leave the world and go to the Father." (NKJ)

Prayer to the Father

John 17:1-5 "When Jesus had spoken these things, He lifted up His eyes to heaven and said, 'Father, the hour has come. Glorify and exalt and honor and magnify Your Son, so that Your Son may glorify and extol and honor and magnify You. [Just as] You have granted Him power and authority over all flesh (all humankind), [now glorify Him] so that He may give eternal life to all whom You have given Him. And this is eternal life: [it means] to know (to perceive, recognize, become acquainted with, and understand) You, the only true and real God, and [likewise] to know Him, Jesus [as the] Christ (the Anointed One, the Messiah), whom You have sent. I have glorified You down here on the earth by completing the work that You gave Me to do. And now, Father, glorify Me along with Yourself and restore Me to such majesty and honor in Your presence as I had with You before the world existed." (AMP)

JESUS' RELATIONSHIP WITH BELIEVERS

Luke 13:34-35 "O Jerusalem, Jerusalem, the city that kills the prophets and stones God's messengers! How often I have wanted to gather your children together as a hen protects her chicks beneath her wings, but you wouldn't let me. And now, look, your house is abandoned. And you will never see me again until you say, 'Blessings on the one who comes in the name of the Lord!'" (NLT)

John 15:14-16 "You are My friends if you do whatever I command you. No longer do I call you servants, for a servant does not know what his master is doing; but I have called you friends, for all things that I heard from My Father I have made known to you. You did not choose Me, but I chose you and appointed you that you should go and bear fruit, and *that* your fruit should remain, that whatever you ask the Father in My name He may give you." (NKJ)

Prayer for His Disciples

John 17:6-19 "I have revealed you to the ones you gave me from this world. They were always yours. You gave them to me, and they have kept your word. Now they know that everything I have is a gift from you, for I have passed on to them the message you gave me. They accepted it and know that I came from you, and they believe you sent me.

My prayer is not for the world, but for those you have given me, because they belong to you. All who are mine belong to you, and you have given them to me, so they bring me glory. Now I am departing from the world; they are staying in this world, but I am coming to you. Holy Father, you have given me your name; now protect them by the power of your name so that they will be united just as we are. During my time here, I protected them by the power of the name you gave me. I guarded them so that not one was lost, except the one headed for destruction, as the Scriptures foretold. Now I am coming to you. I told them many things while I was with them in this world so they would be filled with my joy. I have given them your word. And the world hates them because they do not belong to the world, just as I do not belong to the world. I'm not asking you to take them out of the world, but to keep them safe from the evil one. They do not belong to this world any more than I do. Make them holy by your truth; teach them your word, which is truth. Just as you sent me into the world, I am sending them into the world. And I give myself as a holy sacrifice for them so they can be made holy by your truth." (NLT)

Prayer for All Believers

John 17:20-26 "Neither for these alone do I pray [it is not for their sake only that I make this request], but also for all those who will ever come to believe in (trust in, cling to, rely on) Me through their word and teaching, that they all may be one, [just] as You, Father, are in Me and I in You, that they also may be one in Us, so that the world may believe and be convinced that You have sent Me. I have given to them the glory and honor which You have given Me, that they may be one [even] as We are one: I in them and You in Me, in order that they may become one and perfectly united, that the world may know and [definitely] recognize that You sent Me and that You have loved them [even] as You have loved Me. Father, I desire that they also whom You have entrusted to Me [as Your gift to Me] may be with Me where I am, so that they may see My glory, which You have given Me [Your love gift to Me]; for You loved Me before the foundation of the world. O just and righteous Father, although the world has not known You and has failed to recognize You and has never acknowledged You, I have known You [continually]; and these men understand and know that You have sent Me. I have made Your Name known to them and revealed Your character and Your very Self, and I will continue to make [You] known, that the love which You have bestowed upon Me may be in them [felt in their hearts] and that I [Myself] may be in them." (AMP)

JESUS' MISSION STATEMENTS OF PURPOSE

Luke 4:43 "But He said to them, 'I must preach the kingdom of God to the other cities also, because for this purpose I have been sent.'" (NKJ)

Luke 9:56 "For the Son of Man did not come to destroy men's lives but to save *them...*" (NKJ)

Luke 13:32 "And He said to them, 'Go and tell that fox [sly and crafty, skulking and cowardly], Behold, I drive out demons and perform healings today and tomorrow, and on the third day I finish (complete) My course.'" (AMP)

Luke 19:10 "For the Son of Man has come to seek and to save that which was lost." (NKJ)

John 3:14-15 "And just as Moses lifted up the serpent in the desert [on a pole], so must [so it is necessary that] the Son of Man be lifted up [on the cross], In order that everyone who believes in Him [who cleaves to Him, trusts Him, and relies on Him] may not perish, but have eternal life and [actually] live forever!" (AMP)

John 4:33-34 "Therefore the disciples said to one another, 'Has anyone brought Him anything to eat?' Jesus said to them, 'My food is to do the will of Him who sent Me, and to finish His work.'" (NKJ)

John 12:23,27 "But Jesus answered them, saying, "The hour has come that the Son of Man should be "glorified... Now My soul is troubled, and what shall I say? 'Father, save

Me from this hour'? But for this purpose I came to this hour." (NKJ)

John 14:6 "Jesus said to him, 'I am the way, the truth, and the life. No one comes to the Father except through Me.'" (NKJ)

John 18:37 "Pilate therefore said to Him, 'Are You a king then?' Jesus answered, 'You say *rightly* that I am a king. For this cause I was born, and for this cause I have come into the world, that I should bear witness to the truth. Everyone who is of the truth hears My voice.'" (NKJ)

HOLY SPIRIT

John 14:16-18 "And I will ask the Father, and He will give you another Comforter (Counselor, Helper, Intercessor, Advocate, Strengthener, and Standby), that He may remain with you forever— The Spirit of Truth, Whom the world cannot receive (welcome, take to its heart), because it does not see Him or know and recognize Him. But you know and recognize Him, for He lives with you [constantly] and will be in you. I will not leave you as orphans [comfortless, desolate, bereaved, forlorn, helpless]; I will come [back] to you." (AMP)

John 14:25-26 "These things I have spoken to you while being present with you. But the Helper, the Holy Spirit, whom the Father will send in My name, He will teach you all things, and bring to your remembrance all things that I said to you." (NKJ)

John 15:26 "But when the Comforter (Counselor, Helper, Advocate, Intercessor, Strengthener, Standby) comes, whom I will send to you from the Father, the Spirit of Truth who comes (proceeds) from the Father, He [Himself] will testify regarding Me." (AMP)

John 16:5-15 "But now I am going away to the One who sent me, and not one of you is asking where I am going. Instead, you grieve because of what I've told you. But in fact, it is best for you that I go away, because if I don't, the Advocate won't come. If I do go away, then I will send him to you. And when he comes, he will convict the world of its

107

sin, and of God's righteousness, and of the coming judgment. The world's sin is that it refuses to believe in me.
Righteousness is available because I go to the Father, and
you will see me no more. Judgment will come because the
ruler of this world has already been judged. There is so much
more I want to tell you, but you can't bear it now. When the
Spirit of truth comes, he will guide you into all truth. He will
not speak on his own but will tell you what he has heard.
He will tell you about the future. He will bring me glory by
telling you whatever he receives from me. All that belongs to
the Father is mine; this is why I said, 'The Spirit will tell you
whatever he receives from me.'" (NLT)

John 20:22 "And when He had said this, He breathed on
them, and said to them, 'Receive the Holy Spirit.'" (NKJ)

EXHORTATION, TEACHING, & INSTRUCTION

Matthew 4:4 "But He answered and said, 'It is written, *'Man shall not live by bread alone, but by every word that proceeds from the mouth of God.'*" (NKJ)

Matthew 5:13-16 "You are the salt of the earth. But what good is salt if it has lost its flavor? Can you make it salty again? It will be thrown out and trampled underfoot as worthless. You are the light of the world—like a city on a hilltop that cannot be hidden. No one lights a lamp and then puts it under a basket. Instead, a lamp is placed on a stand, where it gives light to everyone in the house. In the same way, let your good deeds shine out for all to see, so that everyone will praise your heavenly Father." (NLT)

Matthew 6:34 "So do not worry or be anxious about tomorrow, for tomorrow will have worries and anxieties of its own. Sufficient for each day is its own trouble." (AMP)

Matthew 10:27 "Whatever I tell you in the dark, speak in the light; and what you hear in the ear, preach on the housetops." (NKJ)

Matthew 10:29-31 "Are not two little sparrows sold for a penny? And yet not one of them will fall to the ground without your Father's leave (consent) and notice. But even the very hairs of your head are all numbered. Fear not, then; you are of more value than many sparrows." (AMP)

Matthew 11:15 "Anyone with ears to hear should listen and understand." (NLT)

Matthew 12:33-35 "Either make the tree good and its fruit good, or else make the tree bad and its fruit bad; for a tree is known by *its* fruit. Brood of vipers! How can you, being evil, speak good things? For out of the abundance of the heart the mouth speaks. A good man out of the good treasure of his heart brings forth good things, and an evil man out of the evil treasure brings forth evil things." (NKJ)

Parable of the Sower
(Matthew)

Matthew 13:3-23 "He told many stories in the form of parables, such as this one:

'Listen! A farmer went out to plant some seeds. As he scattered them across his field, some seeds fell on a foot-path, and the birds came and ate them. Other seeds fell on shallow soil with underlying rock. The seeds sprouted quickly because the soil was shallow. But the plants soon wilted under the hot sun, and since they didn't have deep roots, they died. Other seeds fell among thorns that grew up and choked out the tender plants. Still other seeds fell on fertile soil, and they produced a crop that was thirty, sixty, and even a hundred times as much as had been planted! Anyone with ears to hear should listen and understand.' His disciples came and asked him, 'Why do you use parables when you talk to the people?' He replied, 'You are permitted to understand the secrets of the Kingdom of Heaven, but others are not. To those who listen to my teaching, more understanding will be given, and they will have an abundance of knowledge. But for those who are not listening, even what little understanding they have will be taken away from them. That is why I use these parables, for they look, but they don't really see. They hear, but they don't really listen or understand. This fulfills the prophecy of Isaiah that says,

'When you hear what I say,
you will not understand.
When you see what I do,
you will not comprehend.
For the hearts of these people are hardened,
and their ears cannot hear,
and they have closed their eyes—
so their eyes cannot see,
and their ears cannot hear,
and their hearts cannot understand,
and they cannot turn to me
and let me heal them.'

But blessed are your eyes, because they see; and your ears, because they hear. I tell you the truth, many prophets and righteous people longed to see what you see, but they didn't see it. And they longed to hear what you hear, but they didn't hear it. Now listen to the explanation of the parable about the farmer planting seeds: The seed that fell on the footpath represents those who hear the message about the Kingdom and don't understand it. Then the evil one comes and snatches away the seed that was planted in their hearts.

The seed on the rocky soil represents those who hear the message and immediately receive it with joy. But since they don't have deep roots, they don't last long. They fall away as soon as they have problems or are persecuted for believing God's word. The seed that fell among the thorns represents those who hear God's word, but all too quickly the message is crowded out by the worries of this life and the lure of wealth, so no fruit is produced. The seed that fell on good soil represents those who truly hear and understand God's word and produce a harvest of thirty, sixty, or even a hundred times as much as had been planted!'" (NLT)

Matthew 14:16 "Jesus said, 'They do not need to go away; you give them something to eat.'" (AMP)

Matthew 16:19 "I will give you the keys of the kingdom of heaven; and whatever you bind (declare to be improper and unlawful) on earth must be what is already bound in heaven; and whatever you loose (declare lawful) on earth must be what is already loosed in heaven." (AMP)

Matthew 16:24-26 "Then Jesus said to His disciples, 'If anyone desires to come after Me, let him deny himself, and take up his cross, and follow Me. For whoever desires to save his life will lose it, but whoever loses his life for My sake will find it. For what profit is it to a man if he gains the whole world, and loses his own soul? Or what will a man give in exchange for his soul?'" (NKJ)

Matthew 18:11-13 "For the Son of man came to save [from the penalty of eternal death] that which was lost. What do you think? If a man has a hundred sheep, and one of them has gone astray and gets lost, will he not leave the ninety-nine on the mountain and go in search of the one that is lost? And if it should be that he finds it, truly I say to you, he rejoices more over it than over the ninety-nine that did not get lost." (AMP)

Parable of the Rich Young Ruler

Matthew 19:16-26 "Someone came to Jesus with this question: 'Teacher, what good deed must I do to have eternal life?' 'Why ask me about what is good?' Jesus replied. 'There is only One who is good. But to answer your question—if you want to receive eternal life, keep the commandments.' 'Which ones?' the man asked. And Jesus replied: 'You must not murder. You must not commit adultery. You must not steal. You must not testify falsely. Honor your father and mother. Love your neighbor as yourself.' 'I've obeyed all these commandments,' the young man replied. 'What else must I do?' Jesus told him, 'If you want to be perfect, go and sell all your possessions and give the money to the poor, and you will have treasure in heaven. Then come, follow me.' But when the young man heard this, he went away sad, for he had many possessions. Then Jesus said to his disciples, 'I tell you the truth, it is very hard for a rich person to enter the Kingdom of Heaven. I'll say it again—it is easier for a camel to go through the eye of a needle than for a rich person to enter the Kingdom of God!' The disciples were astounded. 'Then who in the world can be saved?' they asked. Jesus looked at them intently and said, 'Humanly speaking, it is impossible. But with God everything is possible.'" (NLT)

Matthew 20:25-28 "But Jesus called them to *Himself* and said, 'You know that the rulers of the Gentiles lord it over them, and those who are great exercise authority over them. Yet it shall not be so among you; but whoever desires to become great among you, let him be your servant. And whoever desires to be first among you, let him be your slave— just as the Son of Man did not come to be served, but to serve, and to give His life a ransom for many.'" (NKJ)

Matthew 20:32 "So Jesus stood still and called them, and said, 'What do you want Me to do for you?'" (NKJ)

Matthew 23:8-12 "But you are not to be called Rabbi (teacher), for you have one Teacher and you are all brothers. And do not call anyone [in the church] on earth father, for you have one Father, who is in heaven. And you must not be called masters (leaders), for you have one Master (Leader), the Christ. He who is greatest among you shall be your servant. Whoever exalts himself [with haughtiness and empty pride] shall be humbled (brought low), and whoever humbles himself [whoever has a modest opinion of himself and behaves accordingly] shall be raised to honor." (AMP)

Matthew 26:11 "You will always have the poor among you, but you will not always have me." (NLT)

The Lord's Supper
(Matthew)

Matthew 26:26-29 "Now as they were eating, Jesus took bread and, praising God, gave thanks and asked Him to bless it to their use, and when He had broken it, He gave it to the disciples and said, 'Take, eat; this is My body.' And He took a cup, and when He had given thanks, He gave it to them, saying, 'Drink of it, all of you; For this is My blood of the new covenant, which [ratifies the agreement and] is being poured out for many for the forgiveness of sins. I say to you, I shall not drink again of this fruit of the vine until that day when I drink it with you new and of superior quality in My Father's kingdom.'" (AMP)

Matthew 26:52 "But Jesus said to him, 'Put your sword in its place, for all who take the sword will perish by the sword.'" (NKJ)

The Great Commission

Matthew 28:18-20 "Jesus came and told his disciples, 'I have been given all authority in heaven and on earth. Therefore, go and make disciples of all the nations, baptizing them in the name of the Father and the Son and the Holy Spirit. Teach these new disciples to obey all the commands I have given you. And be sure of this: I am with you always, even to the end of the age.'" (NLT)

Mark 1:17 "Then Jesus said to them, 'Follow Me, and I will make you become fishers of men.'" (NKJ)

Mark 2:14 "And as He was passing by, He saw Levi (Matthew) son of Alphaeus sitting at the tax office, and He said to him, 'Follow Me!' [Be joined to Me as a disciple, side with My party!] And he arose and joined Him as His disciple and sided with His party and accompanied Him." (AMP)

Parable of the Sower
(Mark)

Mark 4:3-20 "Listen! A farmer went out to plant some seed. As he scattered it across his field, some of the seed fell on a footpath, and the birds came and ate it. Other seed fell on shallow soil with underlying rock. The seed sprouted quickly because the soil was shallow. But the plant soon wilted under the hot sun, and since it didn't have deep roots, it died. Other seed fell among thorns that grew up and choked out the tender plants so they produced no grain. Still other seeds fell on fertile soil, and they sprouted, grew, and produced a crop that was thirty, sixty, and even a hundred times as much as had been planted! Then he said, 'Anyone with ears to hear should listen and understand.'

Later, when Jesus was alone with the twelve disciples and with the others who were gathered around, they asked him what the parables meant. He replied, 'You are permitted to understand the secret of the Kingdom of God. But I use parables for everything I say to outsiders, so that the Scriptures might be fulfilled:

'When they see what I do,
they will learn nothing.
When they hear what I say,
they will not understand.
Otherwise, they will turn to me
and be forgiven.'

Then Jesus said to them, 'If you can't understand the meaning of this parable, how will you understand all the other parables? The farmer plants seed by taking God's word to others. The seed that fell on the footpath represents those who hear the message, only to have Satan come at once and take it away. The seed on the rocky soil represents those who hear the message and immediately receive it with joy. But since they don't have deep roots, they don't last long. They fall away as soon as they have problems or are persecuted for believing God's word. The seed that fell among the thorns represents others who hear God's word, but all too quickly the message is crowded out by the worries of this life, the lure of wealth, and the desire for other things, so no fruit is produced. And the seed that fell on good soil represents those who hear and accept God's word and produce a harvest of thirty, sixty, or even a hundred times as much as had been planted!'" (NLT)

Mark 4:21-25 "Also He said to them, 'Is a lamp brought to be put under a basket or under a bed? Is it not to be set on a lampstand? For there is nothing hidden which will not be revealed, nor has anything been kept secret but that it should come to light. If anyone has ears to hear, let him hear.' Then He said to them, 'Take heed what you hear. With the same measure you use, it will be measured to you; and to you who hear, more will be given. For whoever has, to him more will be given; but whoever does not have, even what he has will be taken away from him.'" (NKJ)

Mark 5:36 "As soon as Jesus heard the word that was spoken, He said to the ruler of the synagogue, 'Do not be afraid; only believe.'" (NKJ)

Mark 6:50 "For they all saw Him and were troubled. But immediately He talked with them and said to them, 'Be of good cheer! It is I; do not be afraid.'" (NKJ)

Mark 7:15-19 "There is nothing that enters a man from outside which can defile him; but the things which come out of him, those are the things that defile a man. If anyone has ears to hear, let him hear!' When He had entered a house away from the crowd, His disciples asked Him concerning the parable. So He said to them, 'Are you thus without under-standing also? Do you not perceive that whatever enters a man from outside cannot defile him, because it does not enter his heart but his stomach, and is eliminated, *thus* puri-fying all foods?'" (NKJ)

Mark 8:14-21 "Now the disciples had forgotten to take bread, and they did not have more than one loaf with them in the boat. Then He charged them, saying, 'Take heed, beware of the leaven of the Pharisees and the leaven of Herod.' And they reasoned among themselves, saying,' It is because we have no bread.' But Jesus, being aware of *it,* said to them, 'Why do you reason because you have no bread? Do you not yet perceive nor understand? Is your heart still hardened? Having eyes, do you not see? And having ears, do you not hear? And do you not remember? When I broke the five loaves for the five thousand, how many baskets full of fragments did you take up?' They said to Him, 'Twelve.' 'Also, when I broke the seven for the four thousand, how many large baskets full of fragments did you take up?' And they said, 'Seven.' So He said to them, 'How *is it* you do not understand?'" (NKJ)

Mark 8:34-37 "When He had called the people to *Himself*, with His disciples also, He said to them, 'Whoever desires to come after Me, let him deny himself, and take up his cross, and follow Me. For whoever desires to save his life will lose it, but whoever loses his life for My sake and the gospel's will save it. For what will it profit a man if he gains the whole world, and loses his own soul? Or what will a man give in exchange for his soul?'" (NKJ)

Mark 10:36 "And He said to them, 'What do you want Me to do for you?'" (NKJ)

Mark 12:29-31 "Jesus answered him, 'The first of all the commandments *is: 'Hear, O Israel, the LORD our God, the LORD is one. And you shall love the LORD your God with all your heart, with all your soul, with all your mind, and with all your strength.'* This *is* the first commandment. And the second, like *it, is* this: *'You shall love your neighbor as yourself.'* There is no other commandment greater than these.'" (NKJ)

Mark 14:7 "You will always have the poor among you, and you can help them whenever you want to. But you will not always have me." (NLT)

The Lord's Supper
(Mark)

Mark 14:22-24 "And as they were eating, Jesus took bread, blessed and broke *it,* and gave *it* to them and said, 'Take, eat; this is My body.' Then He took the cup, and when He had given thanks He gave *it* to them, and they all drank from it. And He said to them, 'This is My blood of the new covenant, which is shed for many.'" (NKJ)

Temptation of Jesus in the Wilderness

Luke 4:1-12 "Then Jesus, being filled with the Holy Spirit, returned from the Jordan and was led by the Spirit into the wilderness, being tempted for forty days by the devil. And in those days He ate nothing, and afterward, when they had ended, He was hungry. And the devil said to Him, 'If You are the Son of God, command this stone to become bread.' But Jesus answered him, saying, 'It is written, *'Man shall not live by bread alone, but by every word of God.'*" Then the devil, taking Him up on a high mountain, showed Him all the kingdoms of the world in a moment of time. And the devil said to Him, 'All this authority I will give You, and their glory; for *this* has been delivered to me, and I give it to whomever I wish. Therefore, if You will worship before me, all will be Yours.' And Jesus answered and said to him, 'Get behind Me, Satan! For it is written, *'You shall worship the LORD your God, and Him only you shall serve.'*" Then he brought Him to Jerusalem, set Him on the pinnacle of the temple, and said to Him, 'If You are the Son of God, throw Yourself down from here. For it is written:

> *'He shall give His angels charge over you,*
> *To keep you,'* and,
> *'In their hands they shall bear you up,*
> *Lest you dash your foot against a stone.'"*

And Jesus answered and said to him, 'It has been said, *'You shall not tempt the LORD your God.'"* (NKJ)

Luke 6:39-40 "Then Jesus gave the following illustration: Can one blind person lead another? Won't they both fall into a ditch? Students are not greater than their teacher. But the student who is fully trained will become like the teacher." (NLT)

Luke 6:43-49 "For a good tree does not bear bad fruit, nor does a bad tree bear good fruit. For every tree is known by its own fruit. For *men* do not gather figs from thorns, nor do they gather grapes from a bramble bush. A good man out of the good treasure of his heart brings forth good; and an evil man out of the evil treasure of his heart brings forth evil. For out of the abundance of the heart his mouth speaks. But why do you call Me 'Lord, Lord,' and not do the things which I say? Whoever comes to Me, and hears My sayings and does them, I will show you whom he is like: He is like a man building a house, who dug deep and laid the foundation on the rock. And when the flood arose, the stream beat vehemently against that house, and could not shake it, for it was founded on the rock. But he who heard and did nothing is

like a man who built a house on the earth without a foundation, against which the stream beat vehemently; and immediately it fell. And the ruin of that house was great." (NKJ)

Luke 7:35 "Yet wisdom is vindicated (shown to be true
and divine) by all her children [by their life, character, and
deeds]." (AMP)

Parable of the Sower
(Luke)

Luke 8:5-15 "A sower went out to sow seed; and as he
sowed, some fell along the traveled path and was trodden
underfoot, and the birds of the air ate it up. And some [seed]
fell on the rock, and as soon as it sprouted, it withered
away because it had no moisture. And other [seed] fell in
the midst of the thorns, and the thorns grew up with it and
choked it [off]. And some seed fell into good soil, and grew
up and yielded a crop a hundred times [as great]. As He
said these things, He called out, He who has ears to hear,
let him be listening and let him consider and understand by
hearing!' And when His disciples asked Him the meaning of
this parable, He said to them, 'To you it has been given to
[come progressively to] know (to recognize and understand
more strongly and clearly) the mysteries and secrets of the
kingdom of God, but for others they are in parables, so that,
[though] looking, they may not see; and hearing, they may
not comprehend. Now the meaning of the parable is this:
The seed is the Word of God.

Those along the traveled road are the people who have heard; then the devil comes and carries away the message out of their hearts, that they may not believe (acknowledge Me as their Savior and devote themselves to Me) and be saved [here and hereafter].

And those upon the rock [are the people] who, when they hear [the Word], receive and welcome it with joy; but these have no root. They believe for a while, and in time of trial and temptation fall away (withdraw and stand aloof). And as for what fell among the thorns, these are [the people] who hear, but as they go on their way they are choked and suffocated with the anxieties and cares and riches and pleasures of life, and their fruit does not ripen (come to maturity and perfection). But as for that [seed] in the good soil, these are [the people] who, hearing the Word, hold it fast in a just (noble, virtuous) and worthy heart, and steadily bring forth fruit with patience.'" (AMP)

Luke 8:16-18 "No one lights a lamp and then covers it with a bowl or hides it under a bed. A lamp is placed on a stand, where its light can be seen by all who enter the house.

For all that is secret will eventually be brought into the open, and everything that is concealed will be brought to light and made known to all. So pay attention to how you hear. To those who listen to my teaching, more understanding will be given. But for those who are not listening, even what they think they understand will be taken away from them." (NLT)

Luke 9:23-25 "Then He said to *them* all, 'If anyone desires to come after Me, let him deny himself, and take up his cross daily, and follow Me. For whoever desires to save his life will lose it, but whoever loses his life for My sake will save it. For what profit is it to a man if he gains the whole world, and is himself destroyed or lost?'" (NKJ)

Luke 9:62 "Jesus said to him, 'No one who puts his hand to the plow and looks back [to the things behind] is fit for the kingdom of God.'" (AMP)

Luke 10:9 "And heal the sick there, and say to them, 'The kingdom of God has come near to you.'" (NKJ)

Luke 11:5-10 "Then, teaching them more about prayer, he used this story: Suppose you went to a friend's house at midnight, wanting to borrow three loaves of bread. You say to him, 'A friend of mine has just arrived for a visit, and I have nothing for him to eat.' And suppose he calls out from his bedroom, 'Don't bother me. The door is locked for the night, and my family and I are all in bed. I can't help you.' But I tell you this—though he won't do it for friendship's sake, if you keep knocking long enough, he will get up and give you whatever you need because of your shameless persistence. And so I tell you, keep on asking, and you will receive what you ask for. Keep on seeking, and you will find. Keep on knocking, and the door will be opened to you. For everyone who asks, receives. Everyone who seeks, finds. And to everyone who knocks, the door will be opened." (NLT)

Luke 11:33-36 "No one lights a lamp and then hides it or puts it under a basket. Instead, a lamp is placed on a stand, where its light can be seen by all who enter the house. Your eye is a lamp that provides light for your body. When your eye is good, your whole body is filled with light. But when it is bad, your body is filled with darkness. Make sure that the light you think you have is not actually darkness. If you are filled with light, with no dark corners, then your whole life will be radiant, as though a floodlight were filling you with light." (NLT)

Luke 12:4-7 "I tell you, My friends, do not dread and be afraid of those who kill the body and after that have nothing more that they can do. But I will warn you whom you should fear: fear Him Who, after killing, has power to hurl into hell (Gehenna); yes, I say to you, fear Him! Are not five sparrows sold for two pennies? And [yet] not one of them is forgotten or uncared for in the presence of God. But [even] the very hairs of your head are all numbered. Do not be struck with fear or seized with alarm; you are of greater worth than many [flocks] of sparrows." (AMP)

Luke 12:11-12 "And when they bring you before the synagogues and the magistrates and the authorities, do not be anxious [beforehand] how you shall reply in defense or what you are to say. For the Holy Spirit will teach you in that very hour and moment what [you] ought to say." (AMP)

Luke 12:25 "And which of you by being overly anxious and troubled with cares can add a cubit to his stature or a moment [unit] of time to his age [the length of his life]?" (AMP)

Luke 14:27-33 "And whoever does not bear his cross and come after Me cannot be My disciple. For which of you, intending to build a tower, does not sit down first and count the cost, whether he has *enough* to finish *it*— lest, after he has laid the foundation, and is not able to finish, all who see *it* begin to mock him, saying, 'This man began to build and was not able to finish'? Or what king, going to make war against another king, does not sit down first and consider whether he is able with ten thousand to meet him who comes against him with twenty thousand? Or else, while the other is still a great way off, he sends a delegation and asks conditions of peace. So likewise, whoever of you does not forsake all that he has cannot be My disciple." (NKJ)

Luke 14:34-35 "Salt is good [an excellent thing], but if salt has lost its strength and has become saltless (insipid, flat), how shall its saltness be restored? It is fit neither for the land nor for the manure heap; men throw it away. He who has ears to hear, let him listen and consider and comprehend by hearing!" (AMP)

Luke 16:17 "Yet it is easier for heaven and earth to pass away than for one dot of the Law to fail and become void." (AMP)

Luke 17:7-10 "When a servant comes in from plowing or taking care of sheep, does his master say, 'Come in and eat with me'? No, he says, 'Prepare my meal, put on your apron, and serve me while I eat. Then you can eat later.' And does the master thank the servant for doing what he was told to do? Of course not. In the same way, when you obey me you should say, 'We are unworthy servants who have simply done our duty.'" (NLT)

Luke 20:37-38 "But even Moses showed in the *burning bush passage* that the dead are raised, when he called the Lord *'the God of Abraham, the God of Isaac, and the God of*

Jacob.' For He is not the God of the dead but of the living, for all live to Him." (NKJ)

The Lord's Supper
(Luke)

Luke 22:19-20 "And He took bread, gave thanks and broke *it,* and gave *it* to them, saying, 'This is My body which is given for you; do this in remembrance of Me.' Likewise He also *took* the cup after supper, saying, 'This cup *is* the new covenant in My blood, which is shed for you.'" (NKJ)

Luke 24:25-26 "And [Jesus] said to them, 'O foolish ones [sluggish in mind, dull of perception] and slow of heart to believe (adhere to and trust in and rely on) everything that the prophets have spoken! Was it not necessary and essentially fitting that the Christ (the Messiah) should suffer all these things before entering into His glory (His majesty and splendor)?'" (AMP)

Luke 24:49 "And behold, I will send forth upon you what My Father has promised; but remain in the city [Jerusalem] until you are clothed with power from on high." (AMP)

John 3:12-13 "But if you don't believe me when I tell you about earthly things, how can you possibly believe if I tell you about heavenly things? No one has ever gone to heaven and returned. But the Son of Man has come down from heaven." (NLT)

The Woman at the Well

John 4:7-14 "A woman of Samaria came to draw water. Jesus said to her, 'Give Me a drink.' For His disciples had gone away into the city to buy food. Then the woman of Samaria said to Him, 'How is it that You, being a Jew, ask a drink from me, a Samaritan woman?' For Jews have no dealings with Samaritans. Jesus answered and said to her, 'If you knew the gift of God, and who it is who says to you, 'Give Me a drink,' you would have asked Him, and He would have given you living water.' The woman said to Him, 'Sir, You have nothing to draw with, and the well is deep. Where then do You get that living water? Are You greater than our father Jacob, who gave us the well, and drank from it himself, as well as his sons and his livestock?' Jesus answered and said to her, 'Whoever drinks of this water will thirst again, but whoever drinks of the water that I shall give him will never thirst. But the water that I shall give him will become in him a fountain of water springing up into everlasting life.'" (NKJ)

Jesus the Bread of Heaven

John 6:32-35 "Then Jesus said to them, 'Most assuredly, I say to you, Moses did not give you the bread from heaven, but My Father gives you the true bread from heaven. For the bread of God is He who comes down from heaven and gives life to the world.' Then they said to Him, 'Lord, give us this bread always.' And Jesus said to them, 'I am the bread of life. He who comes to Me shall never hunger, and he who believes in Me shall never thirst. But I said to you that you have seen Me and yet do not believe. All that the Father gives Me will come to Me, and the one who comes to Me I will by no means cast out...' Jesus therefore answered and said to them, 'Do not murmur among yourselves. No one can come to Me unless the Father who sent Me draws him; and I will raise him up at the last day. It is written in the prophets, *'And they shall all be taught by God.'* Therefore everyone who has heard and learned from the Father comes to Me. Not that anyone has seen the Father, except He who is from God; He has seen the Father. Most assuredly, I say to you, he who believes in Me has everlasting life. I am the bread of life. Your fathers ate the manna in the wilderness, and are dead. This is the bread which comes down from heaven, that one may eat of it and not die. I am the living bread which came down from heaven. If anyone eats of this bread, he will live forever; and the bread that I shall give is My flesh, which I shall give for the life of the world.' The Jews therefore quarreled among themselves, saying, 'How can this Man give us *His* flesh to eat?' Then Jesus said to them, 'Most assuredly, I say to you, unless you eat the flesh of the Son of Man and drink His blood, you have no life in you. Whoever eats My flesh and drinks My blood has eternal life, and I will raise him up at the last day. For My flesh is food indeed, and My blood is drink indeed. He who eats My flesh and drinks My blood abides in Me, and I in him. As the living Father sent Me, and I live because of the Father, so he who feeds on Me will live because of Me. This is the bread which came down from heaven—not as your fathers ate the manna, and are dead. He who eats this bread will live forever.'" (NKJ)

John 6:62-65 "What then [will be your reaction] if you should see the Son of Man ascending to [the place] where He was before? It is the Spirit who gives life [He is the Life-giver]; the flesh conveys no benefit whatever [there is no profit in it]. The words (truths) that I have been speaking to you are spirit and life. But [still] some of you fail to believe and trust and have faith. For Jesus knew from the first who did not believe and had no faith and who would betray Him and be false to Him. And He said, 'This is why I told you that no one can come to Me unless it is granted him [unless he is enabled to do so] by the Father.'" (AMP)

John 7:18 "He who speaks on his own authority seeks to win honor for himself. [He whose teaching originates with himself seeks his own glory.] But He Who seeks the glory and is eager for the honor of Him Who sent Him, He is true; and there is no unrighteousness or falsehood or deception in Him." (AMP)

John 7:37-38 "On the last day, that great *day* of the feast, Jesus stood and cried out, saying, 'If anyone thirsts, let him come to Me and drink. He who believes in Me, as the Scripture has said, out of his heart will flow rivers of living water.'" (NKJ)

John 8:12 "Then Jesus spoke to them again, saying, 'I am the light of the world. He who follows Me shall not walk in darkness, but have the light of life.'" (NKJ)

John 8:31-32, 36 "Then Jesus said to those Jews who believed Him, 'If you abide in My word, you are My disciples indeed. And you shall know the truth, and the truth shall make you free... Therefore if the Son makes you free, you shall be free indeed.'" (NKJ)

John 8:50-51 "And though I have no wish to glorify myself, God is going to glorify me. He is the true judge. I tell you the truth, anyone who obeys my teaching will never die!" (NLT)

John 8:58 "Jesus said to them, 'Most assuredly, I say to you, before Abraham was, I AM.'" (NKJ)

John 9:5 "As long as I am in the world, I am the light of the world." (NKJ)

Jesus the Good Shepherd

John 10:1-16 "I tell you the truth, anyone who sneaks over the wall of a sheepfold, rather than going through the gate, must surely be a thief and a robber! But the one who enters through the gate is the shepherd of the sheep. The gatekeeper opens the gate for him, and the sheep recognize his voice and come to him. He calls his own sheep by name and leads them out. After he has gathered his own flock, he walks ahead of them, and they follow him because they know his voice. They won't follow a stranger; they will run from him because they don't know his voice.' Those who heard Jesus use this illustration didn't understand what he meant, so he explained it to them: 'I tell you the truth, I am the gate for the sheep. All who came before me were thieves and robbers. But the true sheep did not listen to them. Yes, I am the gate. Those who come in through me will be saved.

They will come and go freely and will find good pastures. The thief's purpose is to steal and kill and destroy. My purpose is to give them a rich and satisfying life. I am the good shepherd. The good shepherd sacrifices his life for the sheep. A hired hand will run when he sees a wolf coming. He will abandon the sheep because they don't belong to him and he isn't their shepherd. And so the wolf attacks them and scatters the flock. The hired hand runs away because he's working only for the money and doesn't really care about the sheep. I am the good shepherd; I know my own sheep, and they know me, just as my Father knows me and I know the Father. So I sacrifice my life for the sheep. I have other sheep, too, that are not in this sheepfold. I must bring them also. They will listen to my voice, and there will be one flock with one shepherd.'" (NLT)

John 11:9-10 "Jesus answered,' Are there not twelve hours in the day? Anyone who walks about in the daytime does not stumble, because he sees [by] the light of this world.

But if anyone walks about in the night, he does stumble, because there is no light in him' [the light is lacking to him]." (AMP)

John 12:8 "You will always have the poor among you, but you will not always have me." (NLT)

John 12:24-26 "Most assuredly, I say to you, unless a grain of wheat falls into the ground and dies, it remains alone; but if it dies, it produces much grain. He who loves his life will lose it, and he who hates his life in this world will keep it for eternal life. If anyone serves Me, let him follow

Me; and where I am, there My servant will be also. If anyone serves Me, him *My* Father will honor." (NKJ)

John 12:35-36 "Jesus replied, 'My light will shine for you just a little longer. Walk in the light while you can, so the darkness will not overtake you. Those who walk in the darkness cannot see where they are going. Put your trust in the light while there is still time; then you will become children of the light.' After saying these things, Jesus went away and was hidden from them." (NLT)

John 12:44-46 "Then Jesus cried out and said, 'He who believes in Me, believes not in Me but in Him who sent Me. And he who sees Me sees Him who sent Me. I have come *as* a light into the world, that whoever believes in Me should not abide in darkness.'" (NKJ)

Jesus the True Vine

John 15:1-8 "I AM the True Vine, and My Father is the Vinedresser. Any branch in Me that does not bear fruit [that stops bearing] He cuts away (trims off, takes away); and He cleanses and repeatedly prunes every branch that continues to bear fruit, to make it bear more and richer and more excellent fruit. You are cleansed and pruned already, because of the word which I have given you [the teachings I have discussed with you]. Dwell in Me, and I will dwell in you. [Live in Me, and I will live in you.] Just as no branch can bear fruit of itself without abiding in (being vitally united to) the vine, neither can you bear fruit unless you abide in Me. I am the Vine; you are the branches. Whoever lives in Me and

I in him bears much (abundant) fruit. However, apart from Me [cut off from vital union with Me] you can do nothing. If a person does not dwell in Me, he is thrown out like a [broken-off] branch, and withers; such branches are gathered up and thrown into the fire, and they are burned. If you live in Me [abide vitally united to Me] and My words remain in you and continue to live in your hearts, ask whatever you will, and it shall be done for you. When you bear (produce) much fruit, My Father is honored and glorified, and you show and prove yourselves to be true followers of Mine." (AMP)

John 15:18-21 "If the world hates you, know that it hated Me before it hated you.

If you belonged to the world, the world would treat you with affection and would love you as its own. But because you are not of the world [no longer one with it], but I have chosen (selected) you out of the world, the world hates (detests) you. Remember that I told you, a servant is not greater than his master [is not superior to him]. If they persecuted Me, they will also persecute you; if they kept My word and obeyed My teachings, they will also keep and obey yours. But they will do all this to you [inflict all this suffering on you] because of [your bearing] My name and on My account, for they do not know or understand the One Who sent Me." (AMP)

John 20:21b "... As the Father has sent me, so I am sending you." (NLT)

EVANGELISM & TESTIMONY

Mark 1:38 "And He said to them, 'Let us be going on into the neighboring country towns, that I may preach there also; for that is why I came out.'" (AMP)

Mark 5:19 "But Jesus said, 'No, go home to your family, and tell them everything the Lord has done for you and how merciful he has been.'" (NLT)

Mark 6:7,10-12 "And He called to Him the Twelve [apostles] and began to send them out [as His ambassadors] two by two and gave them authority and power over the unclean spirits...And He told them, 'Wherever you go into a house, stay there until you leave that place. And if any community will not receive and accept and welcome you, and they refuse to listen to you, when you depart, shake off the dust that is on your feet, for a testimony against them. Truly I tell you, it will be more tolerable for Sodom and Gomorrah in the judgment day than for that town. So they went out and preached that men should repent' [that they should change their minds for the better and heartily amend their ways, with abhorrence of their past sins]." (AMP)

Mark 16:15 "And He said to them, 'Go into all the world and preach the gospel to every creature.'" (NKJ)

Luke 8:39 "'Return to your own house, and tell what great things God has done for you.' And he went his way and proclaimed throughout the whole city what great things Jesus had done for him." (NKJ)

Luke 10:2 "Then He said to them, 'The harvest truly *is* great, but the laborers *are* few; therefore pray the Lord of the harvest to send out laborers into His harvest.'" (NKJ)

Luke 21:12-15 "But before all these things, they will lay their hands on you and persecute *you,* delivering *you* up to the synagogues and prisons. You will be brought before kings and rulers for My name's sake. But it will turn out for you as an occasion for testimony. Therefore settle *it* in your hearts not to meditate beforehand on what you will answer; for I will give you a mouth and wisdom which all your adversaries will not be able to contradict or resist." (NKJ)

Luke 24:48 "You are witnesses of all these things." (NLT)

John 4:35-38 "Do you not say, 'It is still four months until harvest time comes?' Look! I tell you, raise your eyes and observe the fields and see how they are already white for harvesting. Already the reaper is getting his wages [he who does the cutting now has his reward], for he is gathering fruit (crop) unto life eternal, so that he who does the planting and he who does the reaping may rejoice together. For in this the saying holds true, 'One sows and another reaps.' I sent you to reap a crop for which you have not toiled. Other men have labored and you have stepped in to reap the results of their work." (AMP)

John 5:31-36 "If I were to testify on my own behalf, my testimony would not be valid. But someone else is also testifying about me, and I assure you that everything he says about me is true. In fact, you sent investigators to listen to John the Baptist, and his testimony about me was true. Of course, I have no need of human witnesses, but I say these things so you might be saved. John was like a burning and shining lamp, and you were excited for a while about his message. But I have a greater witness than John—my teachings and my miracles. The Father gave me these works to accomplish, and they prove that he sent me." (NLT)

John 15:27-16:1 "And you also will bear witness, because you have been with Me from the beginning. These things I have spoken to you, that you should not be made to stumble." (NKJ)

MARRIAGE & FAMILY

Matthew 5:31-32 "Furthermore it has been said, 'Whoever divorces his wife, let him give her a certificate of divorce.' But I say to you that whoever divorces his wife for any reason except sexual immorality causes her to commit adultery; and whoever marries a woman who is divorced commits adultery." (NKJ)

Matthew 12:50 "For whoever does the will of My Father in heaven is My brother and sister and mother!" (AMP)

Matthew 18:5-6 "And whoever receives and accepts and welcomes one little child like this for My sake and in My name receives and accepts and welcomes Me. But whoever causes one of these little ones who believe in and acknowledge and cleave to Me to stumble and sin [that is, who entices him or hinders him in right conduct or thought], it would be better (more expedient and profitable or advantageous) for him to have a great millstone fastened around his neck and to be sunk in the depth of the sea." (AMP)

Matthew 18:10 "Take heed that you do not despise one of these little ones, for I say to you that in heaven their angels always see the face of My Father who is in heaven." (NKJ)

Matthew 18:14 "In the same way, it is not my heavenly Father's will that even one of these little ones should perish." (NLT)

Matthew 19:3-12 "The Pharisees also came to Him, testing Him, and saying to Him, 'Is it lawful for a man to divorce his wife for *just* any reason?' And He answered and said to them, 'Have you not read that He who made *them* at the beginning *'made them male and female,'* and said, *'For this reason a man shall leave his father and mother and be joined to his wife, and the two shall become one flesh'*? So then, they are no longer two but one flesh. Therefore what God has joined together, let not man separate.' They said to Him, 'Why then did Moses command to give a certificate of divorce, and to put her away?' He said to them, 'Moses, because of the hardness of your hearts, permitted you to divorce your wives, but from the beginning it was not so. And I say to you, whoever divorces his wife, except for sexual immorality, and marries another, commits adultery; and whoever marries her who is divorced commits adultery.' His disciples said to Him, 'If such is the case of the man with *his* wife, it is better not to marry.' But He said to them, 'All cannot accept this saying, but only *those* to whom it has been given: For there are eunuchs who were born thus from *their* mother's womb, and there are eunuchs who were made eunuchs by men, and there are eunuchs who have made themselves eunuchs for the kingdom of heaven's sake. He who is able to accept *it,* let him accept *it." (NKJ)*

Matthew 19:14 "But Jesus said, 'Let the children come to me. Don't stop them! For the Kingdom of Heaven belongs to those who are like these children.'" (NLT)

Mark 3:33-35 "And He replied, Who are My mother and My brothers? And looking around on those who sat in a circle about Him, He said, 'See! Here are My mother and

My brothers; For whoever does the things God wills is My brother and sister and mother!'" (AMP)

Mark 9:37 "Whoever in My name and for My sake accepts and receives and welcomes one such child also accepts and receives and welcomes Me; and whoever so receives Me receives not only Me but Him Who sent Me." (AMP)

Mark 9:42 "But whoever causes one of these little ones who believe in Me to stumble, it would be better for him if a millstone were hung around his neck, and he were thrown into the sea." (NKJ)

Mark 10:6-9 "But from the beginning of the creation, God *'made them male and female.' 'For this reason a man shall leave his father and mother and be joined to his wife, and the two shall become one flesh'*; so then they are no longer two, but one flesh. Therefore what God has joined together, let not man separate." (NKJ)

Mark 10:11-12 "He told them, "Whoever divorces his wife and marries someone else commits adultery against her. And if a woman divorces her husband and marries someone else, she commits adultery." (NLT)

Mark 10:13-14 "One day some parents brought their children to Jesus so he could touch and bless them. But the disciples scolded the parents for bothering him. When Jesus saw what was happening, He was angry with his disciples. He said to them, 'Let the children come to me. Don't stop them! For the Kingdom of God belongs to those who are like these children.'" (NLT)

Luke 8:20-21 "And it was told Him *by some,* who said, 'Your mother and Your brothers are standing outside, desiring to see You.' But He answered and said to them, 'My mother and My brothers are these who hear the word of God and do it.'" (NKJ)

Luke 9:48 "And said to them, "Whoever receives this little child in My name receives Me; and whoever receives Me receives Him who sent Me. For he who is least among you all will be great." (NKJ)

Luke 11:11-13 "If a son asks for bread from any father among you, will he give him a stone? Or if *he asks* for a fish, will he give him a serpent instead of a fish? Or if he asks for an egg, will he offer him a scorpion? If you then, being evil, know how to give good gifts to your children, how much more will *your* heavenly Father give the Holy Spirit to those who ask Him!" (NKJ)

Luke 20:34-36 "And Jesus said to them, 'The people of this world and present age marry and are given in marriage; But those who are considered worthy to gain that other world and that future age and to attain to the resurrection from the dead neither marry nor are given in marriage; For they cannot die again, but they are angel-like and equal to angels. And being sons of and sharers in the resurrection, they are sons of God.'" (AMP)

BLESSINGS

The Beatitudes

Matthew 5:3-12 "Blessed *are* the poor in spirit, For theirs is the kingdom of heaven.

Blessed *are* those who mourn, For they shall be comforted.

Blessed *are* the meek, For they shall inherit the earth.

Blessed *are* those who hunger and thirst for righteousness, For they shall be filled.

Blessed *are* the merciful, For they shall obtain mercy.

Blessed *are* the pure in heart, For they shall see God.

Blessed *are* the peacemakers, For they shall be called sons of God.

Blessed *are* those who are persecuted for righteousness' sake, For theirs is the kingdom of heaven. Blessed are you when they revile and persecute you, and say all kinds of evil against you falsely for My sake. Rejoice and be exceedingly glad, for great *is* your reward in heaven, for so they persecuted the prophets who were before you." (NKJ)

Matthew 10:41-42 "He who receives and welcomes and accepts a prophet because he is a prophet shall receive a prophet's reward, and he who receives and welcomes and accepts a righteous man because he is a righteous man shall receive a righteous man's reward. And whoever gives to one of these little ones [in rank or influence] even a cup of cold water because he is My disciple, surely I declare to you, he shall not lose his reward." (AMP)

Matthew 11:6 "And blessed is he who is not offended because of Me." (NKJ)

Mark 9:41 "For whoever gives you a cup of water to drink in My name, because you belong to Christ, assuredly, I say to you, he will by no means lose his reward." (NKJ)

Mark 10:28-30 "Then Peter began to say to Him, 'See, we have left all and followed You.' So Jesus answered and said, 'Assuredly, I say to you, there is no one who has left house or brothers or sisters or father or mother or wife or children or lands, for My sake and the gospel's, who shall not receive a hundredfold now in this time—houses and brothers and sisters and mothers and children and lands, with persecutions—and in the age to come, eternal life.'" (NKJ)

Luke 6:20-23 "And solemnly lifting up His eyes on His disciples, He said: Blessed (happy—with life-joy and satis- faction in God's favor and salvation, apart from your outward condition—and to be envied) are you poor and lowly and afflicted (destitute of wealth, influence, position, and honor), for the kingdom of God is yours! Blessed (happy—with life- joy and satisfaction in God's favor and salvation, apart from your outward condition—and to be envied) are you who hunger and seek with eager desire now, for you shall be filled and completely satisfied! Blessed (happy—with life-joy and satisfaction in God's favor and salvation, apart from your outward condition—and to be envied) are you who weep and sob now, for you shall laugh! Blessed (happy—with life-joy and satisfaction in God's favor and salvation, apart from your outward condition—and to be envied) are you when people despise (hate) you, and when they exclude and excommunicate you [as disreputable] and revile and denounce you and defame and cast out and spurn your name as evil (wicked) on account of the Son of Man. Rejoice and be glad at such a time and exult and leap for joy, for behold, your reward is rich and great and strong and intense and abundant in heaven; for even so their forefathers treated the prophets." (AMP)

Luke 7:23 "And blessed (happy—with life-joy and satisfaction in God's favor and salvation, apart from outward conditions—and to be envied) is he who takes no offense in Me and who is not hurt or resentful or annoyed or repelled or made to stumble [whatever may occur]." (AMP)

Luke 11:28 "Jesus replied, "But even more blessed are all who hear the word of God and put it into practice." (NLT)

John 20:27-29"Then He said to Thomas, "Reach your finger here, and look at My hands; and reach your hand *here,* and put *it* into My side. Do not be unbelieving, but believing.' And Thomas answered and said to Him, 'My Lord and my God!' Jesus said to him, 'Thomas, because you have seen Me, you have believed. Blessed *are* those who have not seen and *yet* have believed.'" (NKJ)

PRAYER & FASTING

The Lord's Prayer
(Matthew)

Matthew 6:5-13 "And when you pray, you shall not be like the hypocrites. For they love to pray standing in the synagogues and on the corners of the streets, that they may be seen by men. Assuredly, I say to you, they have their reward. But you, when you pray, go into your room, and when you have shut your door, pray to your Father who *is* in the secret *place;* and your Father who sees in secret will reward you openly. And when you pray, do not use vain repetitions as the heathen *do.* For they think that they will be heard for their many words. Therefore do not be like them. For your Father knows the things you have need of before you ask Him. In this manner, therefore, pray:

Our Father in heaven,
Hallowed be Your name.
Your kingdom come.
Your will be done
On earth as *it is* in heaven.
Give us this day our daily bread.
And forgive us our debts,
As we forgive our debtors.
And do not lead us into temptation,
But deliver us from the evil one.

For Yours is the kingdom and the power and the glory forever. Amen." (NKJ)

Matthew 6:16-18 "Moreover, when you fast, do not be like the hypocrites, with a sad countenance. For they disfigure their faces that they may appear to men to be fasting. Assuredly, I say to you, they have their reward. But you, when you fast, anoint your head and wash your face, so that you do not appear to men to be fasting, but to your Father who *is* in the secret *place;* and your Father who sees in secret will reward you openly." (NKJ)

Matthew 9:15 "And Jesus replied to them, 'Can the wedding guests mourn while the bridegroom is still with them? The days will come when the bridegroom is taken away from them, and then they will fast.'" (AMP)

Matthew 9:37-38 "He said to his disciples, 'The harvest is great, but the workers are few. So pray to the Lord who is in charge of the harvest; ask him to send more workers into his fields.'" (NLT)

Matthew 18:18-20 "Truly I tell you, whatever you forbid and declare to be improper and unlawful on earth must be what is already forbidden in heaven, and whatever you permit and declare proper and lawful on earth must be what is already permitted in heaven.

Again I tell you, if two of you on earth agree (harmonize together, make a symphony together) about whatever [anything and everything] they may ask, it will come to pass and be done for them by My Father in heaven. For wherever two or three are gathered (drawn together as My followers) in (into) My name, there I AM in the midst of them." (AMP)

Matthew 21:22 "And whatever things you ask in prayer, believing, you will receive." (NKJ)

Matthew 26:41 "Keep watch and pray, so that you will not give in to temptation. For the spirit is willing, but the body is weak!" (NLT)

Mark 2:19-22 "Jesus answered them, 'Can the wedding guests fast (abstain from food and drink) while the bridegroom is with them? As long as they have the bridegroom with them, they cannot fast. But the days will come when the bridegroom will be taken away from them, and they will fast in that day. No one sews a patch of unshrunken (new) goods on an old garment; if he does, the patch tears away from it, the new from the old, and the rent (tear) becomes bigger and worse [than it was before]. And no one puts new wine into old wineskins; if he does, the wine will burst the skins, and the wine is lost and the bottles destroyed; but new wine is to be put in new (fresh) wineskins.'" (AMP)

Mark 11:22-24 "So Jesus answered and said to them, "Have faith in God. For assuredly, I say to you, whoever says to this mountain, 'Be removed and be cast into the sea,' and does not doubt in his heart, but believes that those things he says will be done, he will have whatever he says. Therefore I say to you, whatever things you ask when you pray, believe that you receive *them,* and you will have *them.*" (NKJ)

Mark 14:38 "Keep awake and watch and pray [constantly], that you may not enter into temptation; the spirit indeed is willing, but the flesh is weak." (AMP)

Luke 5:33-39 "One day some people said to Jesus, 'John the Baptist's disciples fast and pray regularly, and so do the disciples of the Pharisees. Why are your disciples always eating and drinking?' Jesus responded, 'Do wedding guests fast while celebrating with the groom? Of course not. But someday the groom will be taken away from them, and then they will fast.' Then Jesus gave them this illustration: 'No one tears a piece of cloth from a new garment and uses it to patch an old garment. For then the new garment would be ruined, and the new patch wouldn't even match the old garment. And no one puts new wine into old wineskins. For the new wine would burst the wineskins, spilling the wine and ruining the skins. New wine must be stored in new wineskins. But no one who drinks the old wine seems to want the new wine. 'The old is just fine,' they say.'" (NLT)

Luke 6:28 "Bless those who curse you. Pray for those who hurt you." (NLT)

The Lord's Prayer
(Luke)

Luke 11:2-4 "So He said to them, "When you pray, say:
Our Father in heaven,
Hallowed be Your name.
Your kingdom come.
Your will be done
On earth as *it is* in heaven.
Give us day by day our daily bread.
And forgive us our sins,

For we also forgive everyone who is indebted to us.
And do not lead us into temptation,
But deliver us from the evil one." (NKJ)

Luke 22:40,46 "When He came to the place, He said to them, 'Pray that you may not enter into temptation'...Then He said to them, 'Why do you sleep? Rise and pray, lest you enter into temptation.'" (NKJ)

John 14:13-14 "You can ask for anything in my name, and I will do it, so that the Son can bring glory to the Father. Yes, ask me for anything in my name, and I will do it!" (NLT)

John 15:7 "If you abide in Me, and My words abide in you, you will ask what you desire, and it shall be done for you." (NKJ)

John 16:23-24 "And when that time comes, you will ask nothing of Me [you will need to ask Me no questions]. I assure you, most solemnly I tell you, that My Father will grant you whatever you ask in My Name [as presenting all that I AM]. Up to this time you have not asked a [single] thing in My Name [as presenting all that I AM]; but now ask and keep on asking and you will receive, so that your joy (gladness, delight) may be full and complete." (AMP)

PRAISE & WORSHIP

Matthew 21:16 "and said to Him, 'Do You hear what these are saying?' And Jesus said to them, 'Yes. Have you never read,

'Out of the mouth of babes and nursing infants
You have perfected praise'?'" (NKJ)

Luke 19:40 "But He answered and said to them, 'I tell you that if these should keep silent, the stones would immediately cry out.'" (NKJ)

John 4:22-24 "You worship what you do not know; we know what we worship, for salvation is of the Jews. But the hour is coming, and now is, when the true worshipers will worship the Father in spirit and truth; for the Father is seeking such to worship Him. God *is* Spirit, and those who worship Him must worship in spirit and truth." (NKJ)

PROVISION & PROSPERITY

Matthew 6:25-32 "Therefore I tell you, stop being perpet-ually uneasy (anxious and worried) about your life, what you shall eat or what you shall drink; or about your body, what you shall put on. Is not life greater [in quality] than food, and the body [far above and more excellent] than clothing? Look at the birds of the air; they neither sow nor reap nor gather into barns, and yet your heavenly Father keeps feeding them. Are you not worth much more than they? And who of you by worrying and being anxious can add one unit of measure (cubit) to his stature or to the span of his life? And why should you be anxious about clothes? Consider the lilies of the field and learn thoroughly how they grow; they neither toil nor spin. Yet I tell you, even Solomon in all his magnificence (excellence, dignity, and grace) was not arrayed like one of these. But if God so clothes the grass of the field, which today is alive and green and tomorrow is tossed into the furnace, will He not much more surely clothe you, O you of little faith? Therefore do not worry and be anxious, saying, 'What are we going to have to eat?' or, 'What are we going to have to drink?' or, 'What are we going to have to wear?' For the Gentiles (heathen) wish for and crave and diligently seek all these things, and your heavenly Father knows well that you need them all." (AMP)

Matthew 15:32-38 "Now Jesus called His disciples to *Himself* and said, 'I have compassion on the multitude, because they have now continued with Me three days and have nothing to eat. And I do not want to send them away hungry, lest they faint on the way.' Then His disciples said to Him, 'Where could we get enough bread in the wilderness to fill such a great multitude?' Jesus said to them, 'How many loaves do you have?' And they said, 'Seven, and a few little fish.' So He commanded the multitude to sit down on the ground. And He took the seven loaves and the fish and gave thanks, broke *them* and gave *them* to His disciples; and the disciples *gave* to the multitude. So they all ate and were filled, and they took up seven large baskets full of the fragments that were left. Now those who ate were four thousand men, besides women and children." (NKJ)

Matthew 17:27 "However, we don't want to offend them, so go down to the lake and throw in a line. Open the mouth of the first fish you catch, and you will find a large silver coin. Take it and pay the tax for both of us." (NLT)

Mark 11:2-3 "and He said to them, 'Go into the village opposite you; and as soon as you have entered it you will find a colt tied, on which no one has sat. Loose it and bring *it*. And if anyone says to you, 'Why are you doing this?' say, 'The Lord has need of it,' and immediately he will send it here.'" (NKJ)

Luke 12:22-24 "Then, turning to his disciples, Jesus said, 'That is why I tell you not to worry about everyday life—whether you have enough food to eat or enough clothes to wear. For life is more than food, and your body more than clothing. Look at the ravens. They don't plant or harvest or store food in barns, for God feeds them. And you are far more valuable to him than any birds!'" (NLT)

Luke 12:27-30 "Look at the lilies and how they grow. They don't work or make their clothing, yet Solomon in all his glory was not dressed as beautifully as they are. And if God cares so wonderfully for flowers that are here today and thrown into the fire tomorrow, He will certainly care for you. Why do you have so little faith? And don't be concerned about what to eat and what to drink. Don't worry about such things. These things dominate the thoughts of unbelievers all over the world, but your Father already knows your needs." (NLT)

Luke 22:35 "And He said to them, 'When I sent you without money bag, knapsack, and sandals, did you lack anything?' So they said, 'Nothing.'" (NKJ)

John 21:5-6 "He called out, 'Fellows, have you caught any fish?' 'No,' they replied.

Then he said, 'Throw out your net on the right-hand side of the boat, and you'll get some!' So they did, and they couldn't haul in the net because there were so many fish in it." (NLT)

HEAVEN & HELL & JUDGEMENT

Matthew 6:19-21 "Do not lay up for yourselves treasures on earth, where moth and rust destroy and where thieves break in and steal; but lay up for yourselves treasures in heaven, where neither moth nor rust destroys and where thieves do not break in and steal. For where your treasure is, there your heart will be also." (NKJ)

Matthew 5:21-22 "You have heard that it was said to those of old, *'You shall not murder,* and whoever murders will be in danger of the judgment.' But I say to you that whoever is angry with his brother without a cause shall be in danger of the judgment. And whoever says to his brother, 'Raca!' shall be in danger of the council. But whoever says, 'You fool!' shall be in danger of hell fire." (NKJ)

Matthew 7:1-5 "Do not judge others, and you will not be judged. For you will be treated as you treat others. The standard you use in judging is the standard by which you will be judged. And why worry about a speck in your friend's eye when you have a log in your own? How can you think of saying to your friend, 'Let me help you get rid of that speck in your eye,' when you can't see past the log in your own eye? Hypocrite! First get rid of the log in your own eye; then you will see well enough to deal with the speck in your friend's eye." (NLT)

Matthew 7:13-14 "Enter by the narrow gate; for wide *is* the gate and broad *is* the way that leads to destruction, and there are many who go in by it. Because narrow *is* the gate and difficult *is* the way which leads to life, and there are few who find it." (NKJ)

Matthew 7:21-23 "Not everyone who says to Me, Lord, Lord, will enter the kingdom of heaven, but he who does the will of My Father Who is in heaven. Many will say to Me on that day, 'Lord, Lord, have we not prophesied in Your name and driven out demons in Your name and done many mighty works in Your name?' And then I will say to them openly (publicly), 'I never knew you; depart from Me, you who act wickedly' [disregarding My commands]." (AMP)

Matthew 10:28 "And do not fear those who kill the body but cannot kill the soul. But rather fear Him who is able to destroy both soul and body in hell." (NKJ)

Matthew 10:32-33 "Everyone who acknowledges me publicly here on earth, I will also acknowledge before my Father in heaven. But everyone who denies me here on earth, I will also deny before my Father in heaven." (NLT)

Matthew 12:30-32 "He who is not with Me is against Me, and he who does not gather with Me scatters abroad. Therefore I say to you, every sin and blasphemy will be forgiven men, but the blasphemy *against* the Spirit will not be forgiven men. Anyone who speaks a word against the Son of Man, it will be forgiven him; but whoever speaks against the Holy Spirit, it will not be forgiven him, either in this age or in the *age* to come." (NKJ)

Matthew 12:36-37 "But I say to you that for every idle word men may speak, they will give account of it in the day of judgment. For by your words you will be justified, and by your words you will be condemned." (NKJ)

The Faithful Servant & the Evil Servant

Matthew 24:45-51 "Who then is the faithful, thoughtful, and wise servant, whom his master has put in charge of his household to give to the others the food and supplies at the proper time? Blessed (happy, fortunate, and to be envied) is that servant whom, when his master comes, he will find so doing. I solemnly declare to you, he will set him over all his possessions. But if that servant is wicked and says to himself, My master is delayed and is going to be gone a long time, and begins to beat his fellow servants and to eat and drink with the drunken, the master of that servant will come on a day when he does not expect him and at an hour of which he is not aware, and will punish him [cut him up by scourging] and put him with the pretenders (hypocrites); there will be weeping and grinding of teeth." (AMP)

Matthew 25:34-46 "Then the King will say to those on His right hand, 'Come, you blessed of My Father, inherit the kingdom prepared for you from the foundation of the world: for I was hungry and you gave Me food; I was thirsty and you gave Me drink; I was a stranger and you took Me in; I *was* naked and you clothed Me; I was sick and you visited Me; I was in prison and you came to Me.' Then the righteous will answer Him, saying, 'Lord, when did we see You hungry and feed *You,* or thirsty and give *You* drink? When did we see You a stranger and take *You* in, or naked and clothe *You?* Or when did we see You sick, or in prison, and come to You?' And the King will answer and say to them, 'Assuredly, I say to you, inasmuch as you did *it* to one of the least of these My brethren, you did *it* to Me.' Then He will also say to those on the left hand, 'Depart from Me, you cursed, into the everlasting fire prepared for the devil and his angels: for I was hungry and you gave Me no food; I was thirsty and you gave Me no drink; I was a stranger and you did not take Me in, naked and you did not clothe Me, sick and in prison and you did not visit Me.' Then they also will answer Him, saying, 'Lord, when did we see You hungry or thirsty or a stranger or naked or sick or in prison, and did not minister to You?' Then He will answer them, saying, 'Assuredly, I say to you, inasmuch as you did not do *it* to one of the least of these, you did not do *it* to Me.' And these will go away into everlasting punishment, but the righteous into eternal life." (NKJ)

Mark 9:43-48 "If your hand causes you to sin, cut it off. It is better for you to enter into life maimed, rather than having two hands, to go to hell, into the fire that shall never be quenched— where

'Their worm does not die
And the fire is not quenched.'

And if your foot causes you to sin, cut it off. It is better for you to enter life lame, rather than having two feet, to be cast into hell, into the fire that shall never be quenched- where

'Their worm does not die
And the fire is not quenched.'

And if your eye causes you to sin, pluck it out. It is better for you to enter the kingdom of God with one eye, rather than having two eyes, to be cast into hell fire— where

*'Their worm does not die
And the fire is not quenched.'"* (NKJ)

Mark 16:16 "He who believes [who adheres to and trusts in and relies on the Gospel and Him Whom it sets forth] and is baptized will be saved [from the penalty of eternal death]; but he who does not believe [who does not adhere to and trust in and rely on the Gospel and Him Whom it sets forth] will be condemned." (AMP)

Luke 12:8-10 "Also I say to you, whoever confesses Me before men, him the Son of Man also will confess before the angels of God. But he who denies Me before men will be denied before the angels of God. And anyone who speaks a word against the Son of Man, it will be forgiven him; but to him who blasphemes against the Holy Spirit, it will not be forgiven." (NKJ)

Parable of the Barren Fig Tree

Luke 13:6-9 "Then Jesus told this story: A man planted a fig tree in his garden and came again and again to see if there was any fruit on it, but he was always disappointed. Finally, he said to his gardener, 'I've waited three years, and there hasn't been a single fig! Cut it down. It's just taking up space in the garden.' The gardener answered, 'Sir, give it one more chance. Leave it another year, and I'll give it special attention and plenty of fertilizer. If we get figs next year, fine. If not, then you can cut it down.'" (NLT)

Luke 13:24-30 "Strive to enter through the narrow gate, for many, I say to you, will seek to enter and will not be able. When once the Master of the house has risen up and shut the door, and you begin to stand outside and knock at the door, saying, 'Lord, Lord, open for us,' and He will answer and say to you, 'I do not know you, where you are from,' then you will begin to say, 'We ate and drank in Your presence, and You taught in our streets.' But He will say, 'I tell you I do not know you, where you are from. Depart from Me, all you workers of iniquity.' There will be weeping and gnashing of teeth, when you see Abraham and Isaac and Jacob and all the prophets in the kingdom of God, and yourselves thrust out. They will come from the east and the west, from the north and the south, and sit down in the kingdom of God. And indeed there are last who will be first, and there are first who will be last." (NKJ)

The Rich Man and Lazarus

Luke 16:19-31 "Jesus said, 'There was a certain rich man who was splendidly clothed in purple and fine linen and who lived each day in luxury. At his gate lay a poor man named Lazarus who was covered with sores. As Lazarus lay there longing for scraps from the rich man's table, the dogs would come and lick his open sores. Finally, the poor man died and was carried by the angels to be with Abraham. The rich man also died and was buried, and his soul went to the place of the dead. There, in torment, he saw Abraham in the far distance with Lazarus at his side. The rich man shouted, 'Father Abraham, have some pity! Send Lazarus over here to dip the tip of his finger in water and cool my tongue. I am in anguish in these flames.' But Abraham said to him, 'Son, remember that during your lifetime you had everything you wanted, and Lazarus had nothing. So now he is here being comforted, and you are in anguish. And besides, there is a great chasm separating us. No one can cross over to you from here, and no one can cross over to us from there.' Then the rich man said, 'Please, Father Abraham, at least send him to my father's home. For I have five brothers, and I want him to warn them so they don't end up in this place of torment.' But Abraham said, 'Moses and the prophets have warned them. Your brothers can read what they wrote.' The rich man replied, 'No, Father Abraham! But if someone is sent to them from the dead, then they will repent of their sins and turn to God.' But Abraham said, 'If they won't listen to Moses and the prophets, they won't listen even if someone rises from the dead.'" (NLT)

John 3:18-21 "There is no judgment against anyone who believes in him. But anyone who does not believe in him has already been judged for not believing in God's one and only Son. And the judgment is based on this fact: God's light came into the world, but people loved the darkness more than the light, for their actions were evil. All who do evil hate the light and refuse to go near it for fear their sins will be exposed. But those who do what is right come to the light so others can see that they are doing what God wants." (NLT)

John 12:31 "Now the judgment (crisis) of this world is coming on [sentence is now being passed on this world]. Now the ruler (evil genius, prince) of this world shall be cast out (expelled)." (AMP)

John 12:47-48 "And if anyone hears My words and does not believe, I do not judge him; for I did not come to judge the world but to save the world. He who rejects Me, and does not receive My words, has that which judges him—the word that I have spoken will judge him in the last day." (NKJ)

THE KINGDOM

Matthew 5:19-20 "Whoever therefore breaks one of the least of these commandments, and teaches men so, shall be called least in the kingdom of heaven; but whoever does and teaches *them,* he shall be called great in the kingdom of heaven. For I say to you, that unless your righteousness exceeds *the righteousness* of the scribes and Pharisees, you will by no means enter the kingdom of heaven." (NKJ)

Matthew 6:33 "But seek first the kingdom of God and His righteousness, and all these things shall be added to you." (NKJ)

Parable of the Wheat & Tares

Matthew 13:24-30;36-43 "Here is another story Jesus told: The Kingdom of Heaven is like a farmer who planted good seed in his field. But that night as the workers slept, his enemy came and planted weeds among the wheat, then slipped away. When the crop began to grow and produce grain, the weeds also grew. The farmer's workers went to him and said, 'Sir, the field where you planted that good seed is full of weeds! Where did they come from?' 'An enemy has done this!' the farmer exclaimed. 'Should we pull out the weeds?' they asked. 'No,' he replied, 'you'll uproot the wheat if you do. Let both grow together until the harvest. Then I will tell the harvesters to sort out the weeds, tie them into bundles, and burn them, and to put the wheat in the barn'...Then, leaving the crowds outside, Jesus went into the house. His disciples said, 'Please explain to us the story of the weeds in the field.' Jesus replied, 'The Son of Man is the farmer who plants the good seed. The field is the world, and the good seed represents the people of the Kingdom. The weeds are the people who belong to the evil one. The enemy who planted the weeds among the wheat is the devil. The harvest is the end of the world, and the harvesters are the angels. Just as the weeds are sorted out and burned in the fire, so it will be at the end of the world. The Son of Man will send his angels, and they will remove from his Kingdom everything that causes sin and all who do evil. And the angels will throw them into the fiery furnace, where there will be weeping and gnashing of teeth. Then the righteous will shine like the sun in their Father's Kingdom. Anyone with ears to hear should listen and understand!" (NLT)

Parable of Leaven

Matthew 13:33 "Jesus also used this illustration: The Kingdom of Heaven is like the yeast a woman used in making bread. Even though she put only a little yeast in three measures of flour, it permeated every part of the dough."

Parables of the Hidden Treasure & The Pearl of Great Price

Matthew 13:44-46 "Again, the kingdom of heaven is like treasure hidden in a field, which a man found and hid; and for joy over it he goes and sells all that he has and buys that field. Again, the kingdom of heaven is like a merchant seeking beautiful pearls, who, when he had found one pearl of great price, went and sold all that he had and bought it." (NKJ)

Parable of the Fishing Net

Matthew 13:47-50 "Again, the Kingdom of Heaven is like a fishing net that was thrown into the water and caught fish of every kind. When the net was full, they dragged it up onto the shore, sat down, and sorted the good fish into crates, but threw the bad ones away. That is the way it will be at the end of the world. The angels will come and separate the wicked people from the righteous, throwing the wicked into the fiery furnace, where there will be weeping and gnashing of teeth." (NLT)

Matthew 18:3-4 "And said, Truly I say to you, unless you repent (change, turn about) and become like little children [trusting, lowly, loving, forgiving], you can never enter the kingdom of heaven [at all]. Whoever will humble himself therefore and become like this little child [trusting, lowly, loving, forgiving] is greatest in the kingdom of heaven." (AMP)

Parable of the Workers in the Vineyard

Matthew 20:1-16 "For the Kingdom of Heaven is like the landowner who went out early one morning to hire workers for his vineyard. He agreed to pay the normal daily wage and sent them out to work. At nine o'clock in the morning he was passing through the marketplace and saw some people standing around doing nothing. So he hired them, telling them he would pay them whatever was right at the end of the day. So they went to work in the vineyard. At noon and again at three o'clock he did the same thing. At five o'clock that afternoon he was in town again and saw some more people standing around. He asked them, 'Why haven't you been working today?' They replied, 'Because no one hired us.' The landowner told them, 'Then go out and join the others in my vineyard.'

That evening he told the foreman to call the workers in and pay them, beginning with the last workers first. When those hired at five o'clock were paid, each received a full day's wage. When those hired first came to get their pay, they assumed they would receive more. But they, too, were paid a day's wage. When they received their pay, they protested to the owner, 'Those people worked only one hour, and yet you've paid them just as much as you paid us who worked all day in the scorching heat.' He answered one of them, 'Friend, I haven't been unfair! Didn't you agree to work all day for the usual wage? Take your money and go. I wanted to pay this last worker the same as you. Is it against the law for me to do what I want with my money? Should you be jealous because I am kind to others?' So those who are last now will be first then, and those who are first will be last." (NLT)

Parable of the Two Sons

Matthew 21:28-32 "But what do you think about this? A man with two sons told the older boy, 'Son, go out and work in the vineyard today.' The son answered, 'No, I won't go,' but later he changed his mind and went anyway. Then the father told the other son, 'You go,' and he said, 'Yes, sir, I will.' But he didn't go. Which of the two obeyed his father? They replied, 'The first.' Then Jesus explained his meaning: 'I tell you the truth, corrupt tax collectors and prostitutes will get into the Kingdom of God before you do. For John the Baptist came and showed you the right way to live, but you didn't believe him, while tax collectors and prostitutes did. And even when you saw this happening, you refused to believe him and repent of your sins.'" (NLT)

Parable of the Wedding Feast

Matthew 22:2-14 "The Kingdom of Heaven can be illustrated by the story of a king who prepared a great wedding feast for his son. When the banquet was ready, he sent his servants to notify those who were invited. But they all refused to come! So he sent other servants to tell them, 'The feast has been prepared. The bulls and fattened cattle have been killed, and everything is ready. Come to the banquet!' But the guests he had invited ignored them and went their own way, one to his farm, another to his business. Others seized his messengers and insulted them and killed them. The king was furious, and he sent out his army to destroy the murderers and burn their town. And he said to his servants, 'The wedding feast is ready, and the guests I invited aren't worthy of the honor. Now go out to the street corners and invite everyone you see.' So the servants brought in everyone they could find, good and bad alike, and the banquet hall was filled with guests.

But when the king came in to meet the guests, he noticed a man who wasn't wearing the proper clothes for a wedding. 'Friend,' he asked, 'how is it that you are here without wedding clothes?' But the man had no reply. Then the king said to his aides, 'Bind his hands and feet and throw him into the outer darkness, where there will be weeping and gnashing of teeth.' For many are called, but few are chosen." (NLT)

Parable of the Wise & Foolish Virgins

Matthew 25:1-12 "Then the Kingdom of Heaven shall be likened to ten virgins who took their lamps and went to meet the bridegroom. Five of them were foolish (thoughtless, without forethought) and five were wise (sensible, intelligent, and prudent). For when the foolish took their lamps, they did not take any [extra] oil with them; But the wise took flasks of oil along with them [also] with their lamps. While the bridegroom lingered and was slow in coming, they all began nodding their heads, and they fell asleep. But at midnight there was a shout, 'Behold, the bridegroom! Go out to meet him!' Then all those virgins got up and put their own lamps in order. And the foolish said to the wise, 'Give us some of your oil, for our lamps are going out.' But the wise replied, 'There will not be enough for us and for you; go instead to the dealers and buy for yourselves.' But while they were going away to buy, the bridegroom came, and those who were prepared went in with him to the marriage feast; and the door was shut. Later the other virgins also came and said, 'Lord, Lord, open [the door] to us!' But He replied, 'I solemnly declare to you, I do not know you' [I am not acquainted with you]." (AMP)

Parable of the Talents

Matthew 25:14-30 "Again, the Kingdom of Heaven can be illustrated by the story of a man going on a long trip. He called together his servants and entrusted his money to them while he was gone. He gave five bags of silver to one, two bags of silver to another, and one bag of silver to the last—dividing it in proportion to their abilities. He then left on his trip. The servant who received the five bags of silver began to invest the money and earned five more. The servant with two bags of silver also went to work and earned two more. But the servant who received the one bag of silver dug a hole in the ground and hid the master's money. After a long time their master returned from his trip and called them to give an account of how they had used his money. The servant to whom he had entrusted the five bags of silver came forward with five more and said, 'Master, you gave me five bags of silver to invest, and I have earned five more.' The master was full of praise. 'Well done, my good and faithful servant. You have been faithful in handling this small amount, so now I will give you many more responsibilities. Let's celebrate together!' The servant who had received the two bags of silver came forward and said, 'Master, you gave me two bags of silver to invest, and I have earned two more.' The master said, 'Well done, my good and faithful servant. You have been faithful in handling this small amount, so now I will give you many more responsibilities. Let's celebrate together!' Then the servant with the one bag of silver came and said, 'Master, I knew you were a harsh man, harvesting crops you didn't plant and gathering crops you didn't cultivate. I was afraid I would lose your money, so I hid it in the earth. Look, here is your money back.' But the master replied, 'You wicked and lazy servant! If you knew I harvested crops I didn't plant and gathered crops I didn't cultivate, why didn't you deposit my money in the bank? At least I could have gotten some interest on it.' Then he ordered, 'Take the money from this servant, and give it to the one with the ten bags of silver. To those who use well what they are given, even more will be given, and they will have an abundance. But from those who do nothing, even what little they have will be taken away. Now throw this useless servant into outer darkness, where there will be weeping and gnashing of teeth.'" (NLT)

Mark 1:14-15 "Now after John was put in prison, Jesus came to Galilee, preaching the gospel of the kingdom of God, and saying, 'The time is fulfilled, and the kingdom of God is at hand. Repent, and believe in the gospel.'" (NKJ)

Parable of the Growing Seed

Mark 4:26-29 "Jesus also said, 'The Kingdom of God is like a farmer who scatters seed on the ground. Night and day, while he's asleep or awake, the seed sprouts and grows, but he does not understand how it happens. The earth produces the crops on its own. First a leaf blade pushes through, then the heads of wheat are formed, and finally the grain ripens. And as soon as the grain is ready, the farmer comes and harvests it with a sickle, for the harvest time has come.'" (NLT)

Parable of the Mustard Seed

Mark 4:30-32 "And He said, 'With what can we compare the kingdom of God, or what parable shall we use to illustrate and explain it? It is like a grain of mustard seed, which, when sown upon the ground, is the smallest of all seeds upon the earth; Yet after it is sown, it grows up and becomes the greatest of all garden herbs and puts out large branches, so that the birds of the air are able to make nests and dwell in its shade.'" (AMP)

Mark 10:15 "Assuredly, I say to you, whoever does not receive the kingdom of God as a little child will by no means enter it." (NKJ)

Mark 10:23-25 "And Jesus looked around and said to His disciples, 'With what difficulty will those who possess wealth and keep on holding it enter the kingdom of God' And the disciples were amazed and bewildered and perplexed at His words. But Jesus said to them again, 'Children, how hard it is for those who trust (place their confidence, their sense of safety) in riches to enter the kingdom of God! It is easier for a camel to go through the eye of a needle than for a rich man to enter the kingdom of God.'" (AMP)

Luke 7:28 "For I say to you, among those born of women there is not a greater prophet than John the Baptist; but he who is least in the kingdom of God is greater than he." (NKJ)

Luke 12:31-32 "But seek the kingdom of God, and all these things shall be added to you. Do not fear, little flock, for it is your Father's good pleasure to give you the kingdom." (NKJ)

Luke 16:16 "The law and the prophets *were* until John. Since that time the kingdom of God has been preached, and everyone is pressing into it." (NKJ)

Luke 17:20-21 "Now when He was asked by the Pharisees when the kingdom of God would come, He answered them and said, 'The kingdom of God does not come with observation; nor will they say, 'See here!' or 'See there!' For indeed, the kingdom of God is within you.'" (NKJ)

Luke 18:16-17 "Then Jesus called for the children and said to the disciples, 'Let the children come to me. Don't stop them! For the Kingdom of God belongs to those who are like these children. I tell you the truth, anyone who doesn't receive the Kingdom of God like a child will never enter it.'" (NLT)

Luke 18:24-25 "And when Jesus saw that he became very sorrowful, He said, 'How hard it is for those who have riches to enter the kingdom of God! For it is easier for a camel to go through the eye of a needle than for a rich man to enter the kingdom of God.'" (NKJ)

Parable of the Ten Servants

Luke 19:11-26 "The crowd was listening to everything Jesus said. And because he was nearing Jerusalem, He told them a story to correct the impression that the Kingdom of God would begin right away. He said, 'A nobleman was called away to a distant empire to be crowned king and then return. Before he left, he called together ten of his servants and divided among them ten pounds of silver, saying, 'Invest this for me while I am gone.' But his people hated him and sent a delegation after him to say, 'We do not want him to be our king.' After he was crowned king, he returned and called in the servants to whom he had given the money. He wanted to find out what their profits were. The first servant reported, 'Master, I invested your money and made ten times the original amount!' 'Well done!' the king exclaimed. 'You are a good servant. You have been faithful with the little I entrusted to you, so you will be governor of ten cities as your reward.' The next servant reported, 'Master, I invested your money and made five times the original amount.' 'Well done!' the king said. 'You will be governor over five cities.'

But the third servant brought back only the original amount of money and said, 'Master, I hid your money and kept it safe. I was afraid because you are a hard man to deal with, taking what isn't yours and harvesting crops you didn't plant.' 'You wicked servant!' the king roared. 'Your own words condemn you. If you knew that I'm a hard man who takes what isn't mine and harvests crops I didn't plant, why didn't you deposit my money in the bank? At least I could have gotten some interest on it.' Then, turning to the others standing nearby, the king ordered, 'Take the money from this servant, and give it to the one who has ten pounds.' 'But, master,' they said, 'he already has ten pounds!' 'Yes,' the king replied, 'and to those who use well what they are given, even more will be given. But from those who do nothing, even what little they have will be taken away." (NLT)

Luke 22:28-30 "And you are those who have remained [throughout] and persevered with Me in My trials; And as My Father has appointed a kingdom and conferred it on Me, so do I confer on you [the privilege and decree], that you may eat and drink at My table in My kingdom and sit on thrones, judging the twelve tribes of Israel." (AMP)

John 18:36 "Jesus answered, "My kingdom is not of this world. If My kingdom were of this world, My servants would fight, so that I should not be delivered to the Jews; but now My kingdom is not from here." (NKJ)

THE SECOND COMING

Matthew 16:27 "For the Son of Man is going to come in the glory (majesty, splendor) of His Father with His angels, and then He will render account and reward every man in accordance with what he has done." (AMP)

Matthew 25:13 "Watch therefore, for you know neither the day nor the hour in which the Son of Man is coming." (NKJ)

Matthew 25:31-33 "But when the Son of Man comes in his glory, and all the angels with him, then he will sit upon his glorious throne. All the nations will be gathered in his presence, and he will separate the people as a shepherd separates the sheep from the goats. He will place the sheep at his right hand and the goats at his left." (NLT)

Matthew 26:63-64 "But Jesus kept silent. And the high priest answered and said to Him, 'I put You under oath by the living God: Tell us if You are the Christ, the Son of God!' Jesus said to him, '*It is as* you said. Nevertheless, I say to you, hereafter you will see the Son of Man sitting at the right hand of the Power, and coming on the clouds of heaven.'" (NKJ)

Mark 8:38 "For whoever is ashamed [here and now] of Me and My words in this adulterous (unfaithful) and [preeminently] sinful generation, of him will the Son of Man also be ashamed when He comes in the glory (splendor and majesty) of His Father with the holy angels." (AMP)

Mark 13:24-27 "But in those days, after that tribulation, the sun will be darkened, and the moon will not give its light; the stars of heaven will fall, and the powers in the heavens will be shaken. Then they will see the Son of Man coming in the clouds with great power and glory. And then He will send His angels, and gather together His elect from the four winds, from the farthest part of earth to the farthest part of heaven." (NKJ)

Mark 14:62 "And Jesus said, 'I AM; and you will [all] see the Son of Man seated at the right hand of Power (the Almighty) and coming on the clouds of heaven'" (AMP)

Luke 9:26 "If anyone is ashamed of me and my message, the Son of Man will be ashamed of that person when he returns in his glory and in the glory of the Father and the holy angels." (NLT)

Luke 12:35-48 "Be dressed for service and keep your lamps burning, as though you were waiting for your master to return from the wedding feast. Then you will be ready to open the door and let him in the moment he arrives and knocks. The servants who are ready and waiting for his return will be rewarded. I tell you the truth, he himself will seat them, put on an apron, and serve them as they sit and eat! He may come in the middle of the night or just before dawn. But whenever he comes, he will reward the servants who are ready. Understand this: If a homeowner knew exactly when a burglar was coming, he would not permit his house to be broken into. You also must be ready all the time, for the Son of Man will come when least expected. Peter asked, 'Lord, is that illustration just for us or for everyone?' And the Lord replied, 'A faithful, sensible servant is one to whom the master can give the responsibility of managing his other household servants and feeding them. If the master returns and finds that the servant has done a good job, there will be a reward. I tell you the truth, the master will put that servant in charge of all he owns. But what if the servant thinks, 'My master won't be back for a while,' and he begins beating the other servants, partying, and getting drunk- The master will return unannounced and unexpected, and he will cut the servant in pieces and banish him with the unfaithful. And a servant who knows what the master wants, but isn't prepared and doesn't carry out those instructions, will be severely punished. But someone who does not know, and then does something wrong, will be punished only lightly. When someone has been given much, much will be required in return; and when someone has been entrusted with much, even more will be required.'" (NLT)

Parable of the Great Supper

Luke 14:16-24 "Jesus replied with this story: A man prepared a great feast and sent out many invitations. When the banquet was ready, he sent his servant to tell the guests, 'Come, the banquet is ready.' But they all began making excuses. One said, 'I have just bought a field and must inspect it. Please excuse me.' Another said, 'I have just bought five pairs of oxen, and I want to try them out. Please excuse me.' Another said, 'I now have a wife, so I can't come.' The servant returned and told his master what they had said. His master was furious and said, 'Go quickly into the streets and alleys of the town and invite the poor, the crippled, the blind, and the lame.' After the servant had done this, he reported, 'There is still room for more.' So his master said, 'Go out into the country lanes and behind the hedges and urge anyone you find to come, so that the house will be full. For none of those I first invited will get even the smallest taste of my banquet.'" (NLT)

Luke 18:8b "...Nevertheless, when the Son of Man comes, will He really find faith on the earth?" (NKJ)

Luke 21:25-28 "And there will be signs in the sun and moon and stars; and upon the earth [there will be] distress (trouble and anguish) of nations in bewilderment and perplexity [without resources, left wanting, embarrassed, in doubt, not knowing which way to turn] at the roaring (the echo) of the tossing of the sea, men swooning away or expiring with fear and dread and apprehension and expectation of the things that are coming on the world; for the [very] powers of the heavens will be shaken and caused to totter. And then they will see the Son of Man coming in a cloud with great (transcendent and overwhelming) power and [all His kingly] glory (majesty and splendor). Now when these things begin to occur, look up and lift up your heads, because your redemption (deliverance) is drawing near." (AMP)

Luke 21:34-36 "But take heed to yourselves, lest your hearts be weighed down with carousing, drunkenness, and cares of this life, and that Day come on you unexpectedly. For it will come as a snare on all those who dwell on the face of the whole earth. Watch therefore, and pray always that you may be counted worthy to escape all these things that will come to pass, and to stand before the Son of Man." (NKJ)

John 5:25,28-29 "Believe Me when I assure you, most solemnly I tell you, the time is coming and is here now when the dead shall hear the voice of the Son of God and those who hear it shall live...Do not be surprised and wonder at this, for the time is coming when all those who are in the tombs shall hear His voice, and they shall come out—those who have practiced doing good [will come out] to the resurrection of [new] life, and those who have done evil will be raised for judgment [raised to meet their sentence]." (AMP)

John 14:2-3 "In My Father's house are many mansions; if *it were* not *so,* I would have told you. I go to prepare a place for you. And if I go and prepare a place for you, I will come again and receive you to Myself; that where I am, *there* you may be also. (NKJ)

CONCLUSION

W hat do you need in your life today? Whatever you are facing, you need to know and understand that Jesus is the answer. Ask Jesus to help you. He is willing to release His power to do what only He can do, but you must first ask.

Jesus understands what you are going through. Jesus suffered many terrible things while here on earth. He was lied about, betrayed by friends, and was eventually killed by crucifixion even though he was completely innocent and never committed a sin. But by the power of the Holy Spirit, he arose from the dead three days later and had complete victory. You can have that same overcoming power in your life by allowing Jesus to be your Savior and Lord of your life.

The penalty of any sin is death. Since all of us have sinned, we deserve the punishment of death because God is Holy. But through His death, Jesus took our place. He took all the sin of all mankind upon himself. He chose to do this because He loves you and me so much and Jesus wants us to have fellowship with Father God. Jesus said "No man takes my life. I lay it down willingly." - John 10:18

Through my own trials I have learned never to question the heart of God and His goodness. He is always good. Contend in faith to see the promises of God come to pass in your life. Set yourself in agreement with the Word of God and not the word of man or the enemy of your soul. The Word of God is always true no matter how we feel or whatever our circumstances. The Word is a higher level of truth than our present reality. "Let God be true and every man a liar" - Romans 3:4

God hears you. He is listening. Ask Him to help you.

Are you sick with disease or injury?

By the stripes of Jesus, you are healed - Isaiah 53:5
He heals all of your diseases - Psalm 103:1-3
He sent His Word and healed you - Psalm 107:20

Is there strife and fighting in your home?

Jesus gives you special, supernatural peace not found normally in the world - John 14:27
For Jesus Himself is your peace - Ephesians 2:14
Keep your mind focused on Jesus, trust Him, and He will keep you in perfect peace - Isaiah 26:3

Do you need finances?

Jesus is your portion - Psalm 16:5

The Lord delights in the prosperity of His servants - Psalm 35:27

The Lord will bless and establish the work of your hands - Psalm 90:17

Do you need freedom from sin, bondages, and addictions?

In Jesus, you are no longer bound or enslaved to sin but set free to life - Romans 6:22

Jesus gives you the power to overcome any addiction - Luke 10:19

When Jesus makes you free you are truly free indeed - John 8:36

Are you tired and weary?

If you are burdened, come to Jesus and He will give you rest - Matthew 11:28-30

Wait on the Lord and He will give you new strength. You will run and not be weary - Isaiah 40:31

Tell Jesus about your troubles and burdens and He will sustain you - Psalm 55:22

Do you need help with decisions?

If you lack wisdom, then ask God who gives freely - James 1:5

The fear of the Lord is the beginning of wisdom - Psalm 111:10

It is the Lord that gives you wisdom, knowledge, and understanding - Proverbs 2:6

Are you confused and frustrated with life?

God is not the author of confusion - 1 Corinthians 14:33

God replaces confusion with rejoicing and shame for double honor - Isaiah 61:7

God will restore your honor and whatever has been taken from you - Nahum 2:2

Are you depressed or discouraged?

Don't be anxious or worried about anything, but tell Jesus about your problems because He cares about you - Philippians 4:6

God will lift you out of the pit of despair and set you on solid ground - Psalm 40:2

God will replace your despair with praise and your mourning with joyful blessing - Isaiah 61:3

Do you need a goal or a vision for your life?

God has good plans for you. Plans never to harm you but to make you prosper and to give you hope for your future - Jeremiah 29:11
Commit to the Lord whatever you do and your plans will succeed - Proverbs 16:3
Wise counselors are needed to establish your plans - Proverbs 15:22

Do you need salvation?

There is no other name given among men by which you must be saved but the name of Jesus - Acts 4:12.
If you believe in your heart and confess with your mouth that Jesus is Lord then you will be saved - Romans 10:10
You are saved by grace through faith in Jesus, not by what you do. Salvation is a gift from God to you - Ephesians 2:8

If you would like Jesus to come into your heart and change your life, cleanse you from all you've done wrong and all your sin, then pray this prayer from your heart. Speak these words out loud when you pray:

Father, I come to you knowing I am a sinner and I have done things that were wrong and not pleasing to you. Please forgive me for all the bad things I've done and the good things I've failed to do. Cleanse me of all my sin by the blood of Jesus. Come into my heart and my life and change me into the person you want me to be. Jesus, fill me with your Holy Spirit to empower me to do what is right. Fill me with the fullness of your love, your peace, your joy, your healing, your deliverance, your strength, your victory, and your overcoming power. Jesus, because you have redeemed my life and because of your great love for me, I commit my life to serving and honoring you. Thank you for the gift of yourself and for changing my life right now and for all eternity.

In Jesus name,

Amen

CPSIA information can be obtained at www.ICGtesting.com
Printed in the USA
LVOW061315281112

309064LV00001B/186/P